T0033962

BUILDING BASS DRUM TECHNIQUE

Strength, Speed, Endurance, And Control For Single Bass Drum Players

By Ron Spagnardi

Design And Layout By Joe King

© Copyright 2001 Modern Drummer Publications, Inc.

International Copyright Secured

All Rights Reserved

Any unauthorized duplication of this book or
its contents is a violation of copyright laws.

Published By
Modern Drummer Publications, Inc.
12 Old Bridge Road
Cedar Grove, NJ 07009 USA

Table Of Contents

Introduction

Building Bass Drum Technique has been written for single bass drum players who wish to develop a greater level of bass drum foot strength, speed, endurance, and control.

Though many of today's drummers have opted for double bass drums and double bass pedals, an equally large number have remained with the traditional single bass drum setup. Development of the foot on a single bass drum can present quite a different challenge from double bass drums or double pedals. This book has been written to help the single bass drum player attain the most effective and efficient results.

Building Bass Drum Technique is designed in a very simple, methodical manner. The book's eight sections offer bass drum development exercises using 8th notes, triplets, two common 16th-note figures, straight 16th notes, 16th-note triplets, and 32nd notes.

Each section of the book is divided into five parts. Part 1 presents a speed and endurance program with an accompanying progress chart. Part 2 is a study in the use of accents with the foot. Part 3 offers a solo using bass drum alone. In Part 4 a selection of hand and foot patterns helps to further develop bass drum speed, control, and hand/foot coordination. Part 5 is a summary of the entire section with a solo that further enhances the hand and foot reflex action.

Finally, in the last section of the book, five challenging solos are presented using combinations of the previously studied material.

Though recommendations for the most efficient use of these lessons are stated many times throughout the text, let's go over them now to get you started "on the right foot":

1) Begin each new section of the book at a comfortable tempo. *Do not* attempt to play the exercises too fast at the onset. Speed will come gradually with regular practice.

2) Use a metronome or drum machine to ensure a steady, even time flow and to keep a record of your progress.

3) Repeat all 8th-note and 8th-note triplet exercises *ten* to *twenty* times before moving on. Repeat both 16th-note figures, straight 16th notes, 16th-note triplets, and 32nd-note exercises *five* to *ten* times before moving on. Rest between each exercise as needed.

4) Gradually increase the tempo as you become more fluent with the exercises in each section.

5) The accents in Part 4 of each section add rhythmic interest to each exercise. However, they are optional and can be added later after the hand/foot patterns have been mastered.

6) Practice all sections of the book using both the *heel up* and *heel down* bass drum pedal technique.

Though some of the material in this book may initially appear quite difficult, don't become discouraged. Give yourself ample time for your bass drum foot to gradually develop through regular practice. Follow the guidelines above, devote serious practice time to everything presented here, and you'll soon be amazed at the level of strength, speed, control, and endurance you'll acquire with *Building Bass Drum Technique*.

Section 1

Part 1: 8th-Note Speed And Endurance Exercise

The purpose of Part 1 is to help you develop a greater degree of bass drum speed and endurance. Using straight 8th notes, and starting at a comfortable tempo, play as many measures of 8th notes as you can. Do not push to the point of cramping or burning. Stop when you can no longer control a full measure of 8th notes.

On the Endurance Progress Chart below, you can keep a record of your progress on a daily or weekly basis in the Date column.

Start at a comfortable tempo and write that tempo down under the M.M. (metronome marking) column.

As you play each measure of 8th notes, count out the total number of measures you are able to play without stopping, and mark it down in the Measures column.

The idea is to gradually increase both the speed (M.M.) and the number of measures you can play at that speed with each practice session. At the onset, *do not* attempt to play at a tempo faster than you're capable of playing. *Do not* attempt to play more measures than you can comfortably play. Foot speed, endurance, and control come with relaxed muscle action and gradual, consistent practice.

ENDURANCE PROGRESS CHART

Date	M.M.	# Of Measures

Part 2: 8th Notes With Accents

The first step for developing better bass drum technique is by practicing 8th notes with accents. Be sure to play the unaccented notes much lighter than the accented ones, and keep a steady, even tempo. Use a metronome or a drum machine, and gradually increase the tempo as you master each exercise. Repeat each pattern ten to twenty times without stopping before moving on to the next one. Also, be sure to practice all of the patterns with your heel up *and* down.

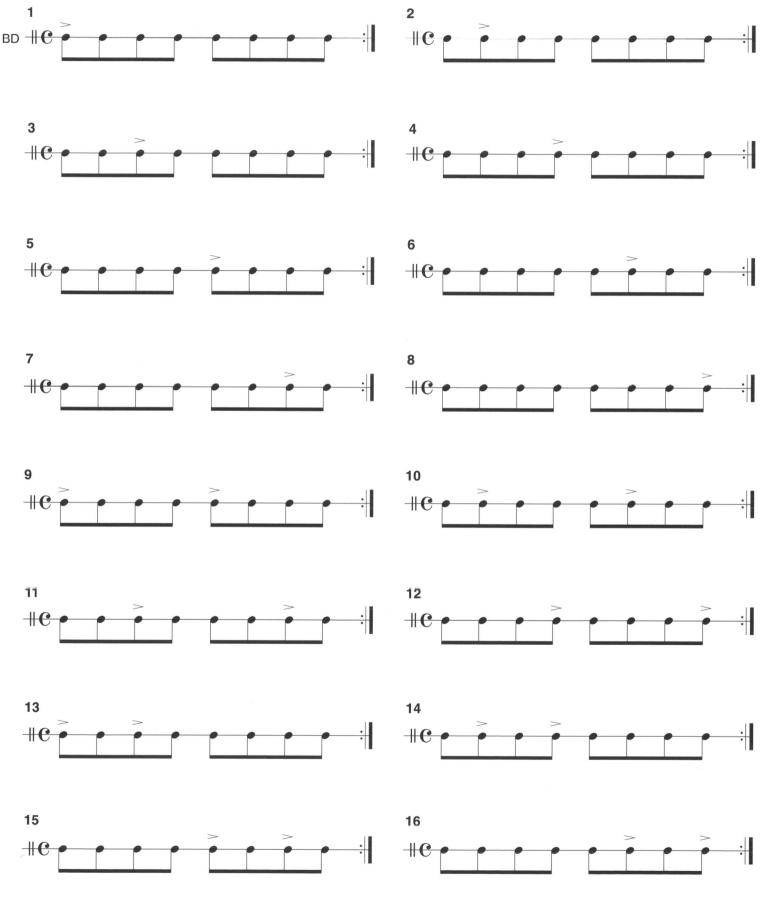

5

17

BD

18

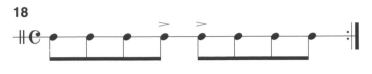

19

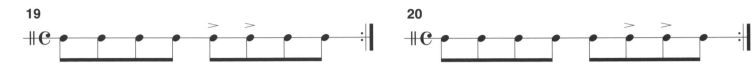

20

21

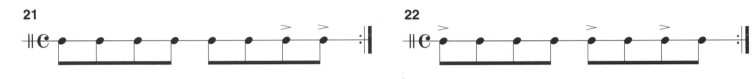

22

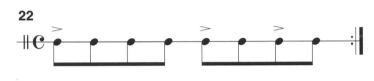

23

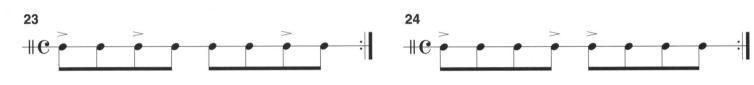

24

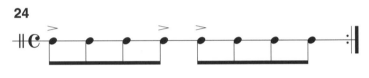

25

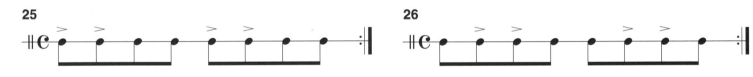

26

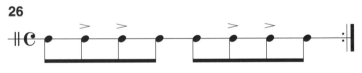

27

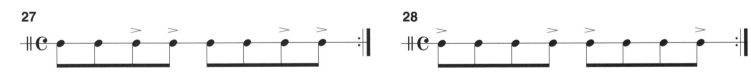

28

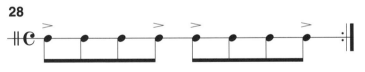

29

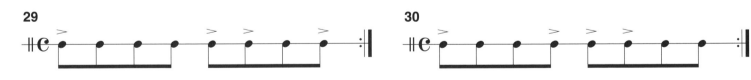

30

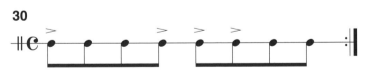

31

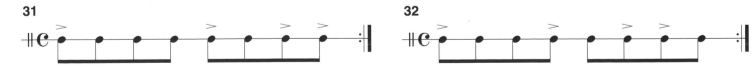

32

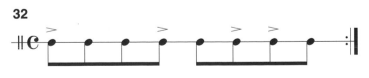

33

BD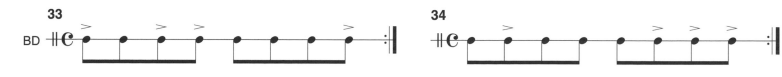

34

35

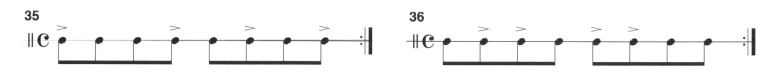

36

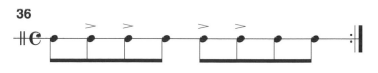

37

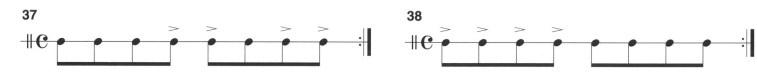

38

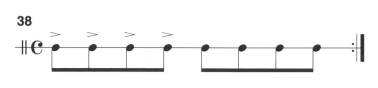

39

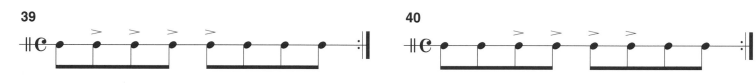

40

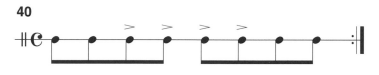

41

42

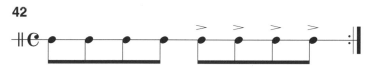

43

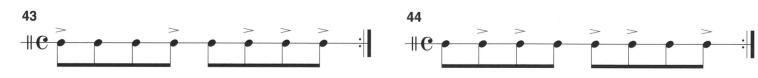

44

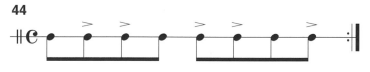

45

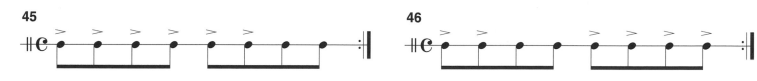

46

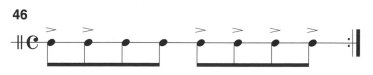

47

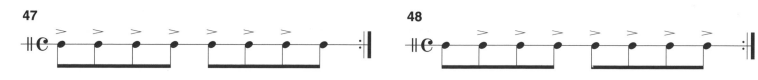

48

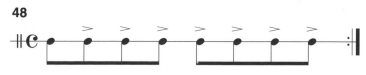

Part 3: 8th-Note Bass Drum Solo

Part 3 is a bass drum solo utilizing 8th notes and quarter notes. Be sure to play the accented notes stronger than the non-accented ones. Start slowly, increase the tempo gradually, and use a metronome or drum machine to keep a record of your progress.

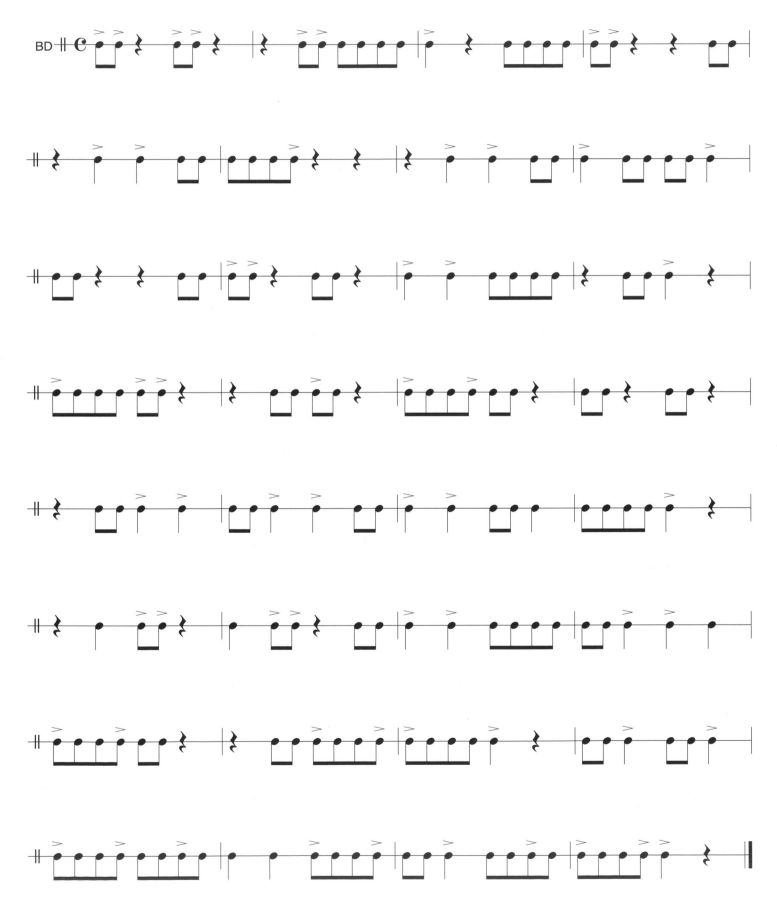

Part 4: 8th-Note Hand And Foot Patterns

The next four pages involve hand and foot patterns with 8th notes. Master each one before proceeding to the next. Begin slowly, and gradually increase the tempo as you become more familiar with each pattern. Also, be sure to practice the exercises heel up and heel down.

The accents, indicated in parentheses, are optional and add extra rhythmic interest to each exercise. Another option is to randomly move the hand part around to the various drums and cymbals on your kit. This is an excellent means of developing more facility around the set, as well as increasing foot strength and control.

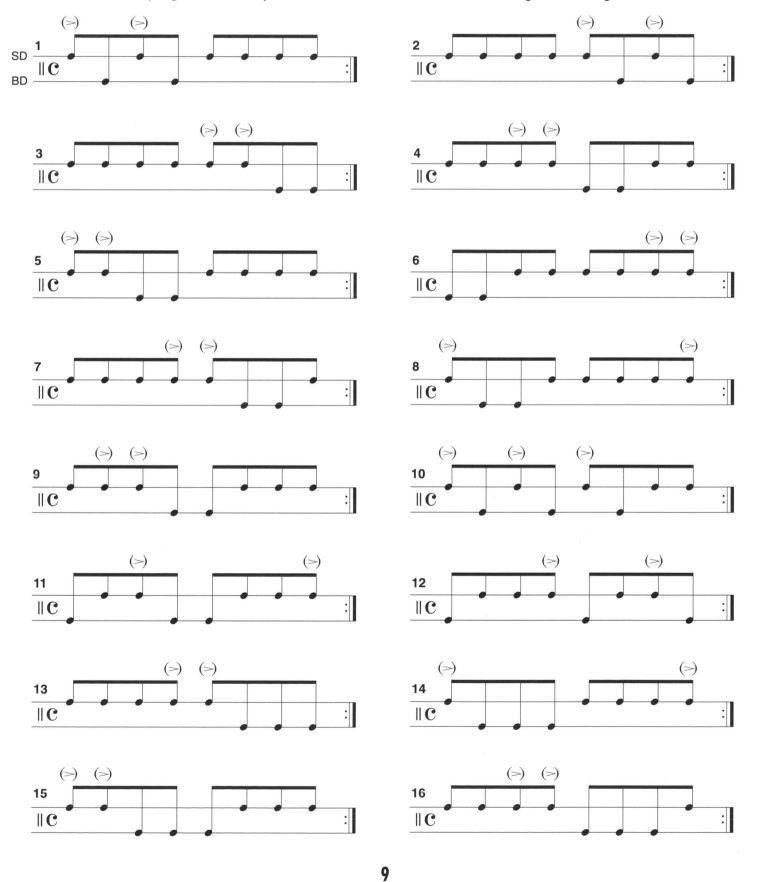

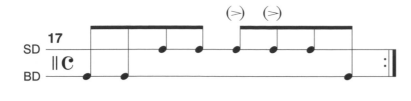

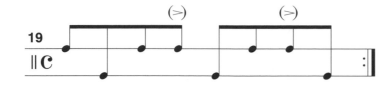

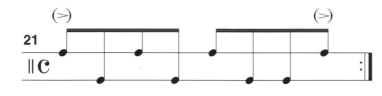

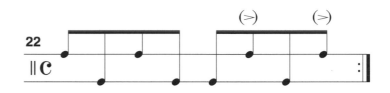

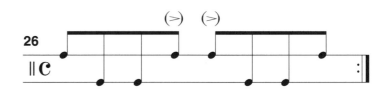

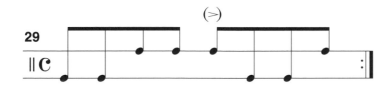

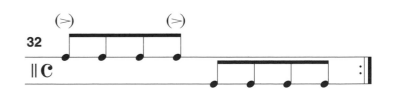

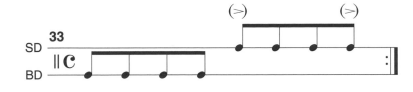

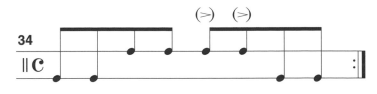

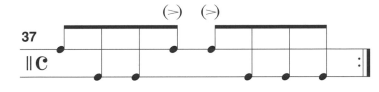

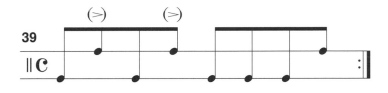

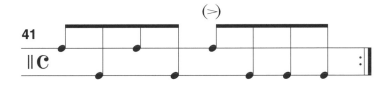

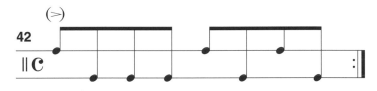

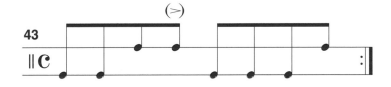

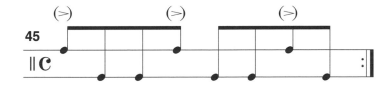

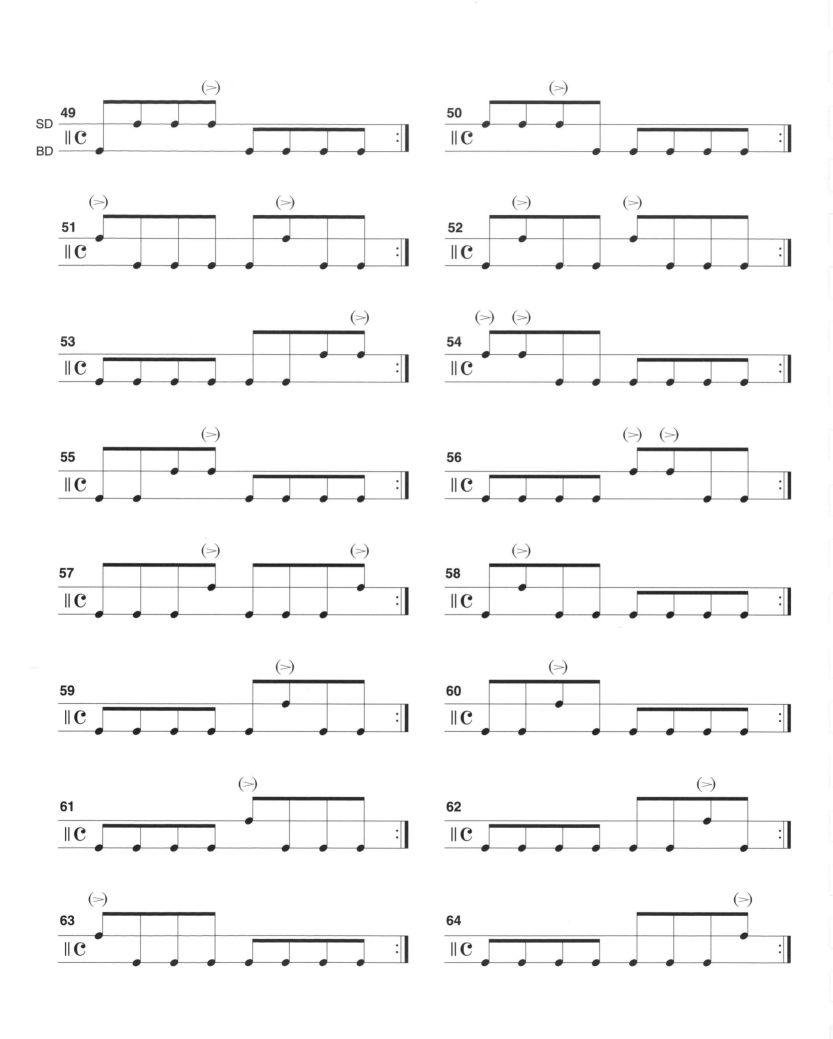

Part 5: 8th-Note Hand And Foot Solo

Here's a thirty-two-bar solo using most of the hand and foot patterns from the previous pages, with the addition of accents. Practice this solo slowly, and increase the speed as you become more familiar with the material. Your ultimate goal should be to play the solo from beginning to end without stopping and without an error.

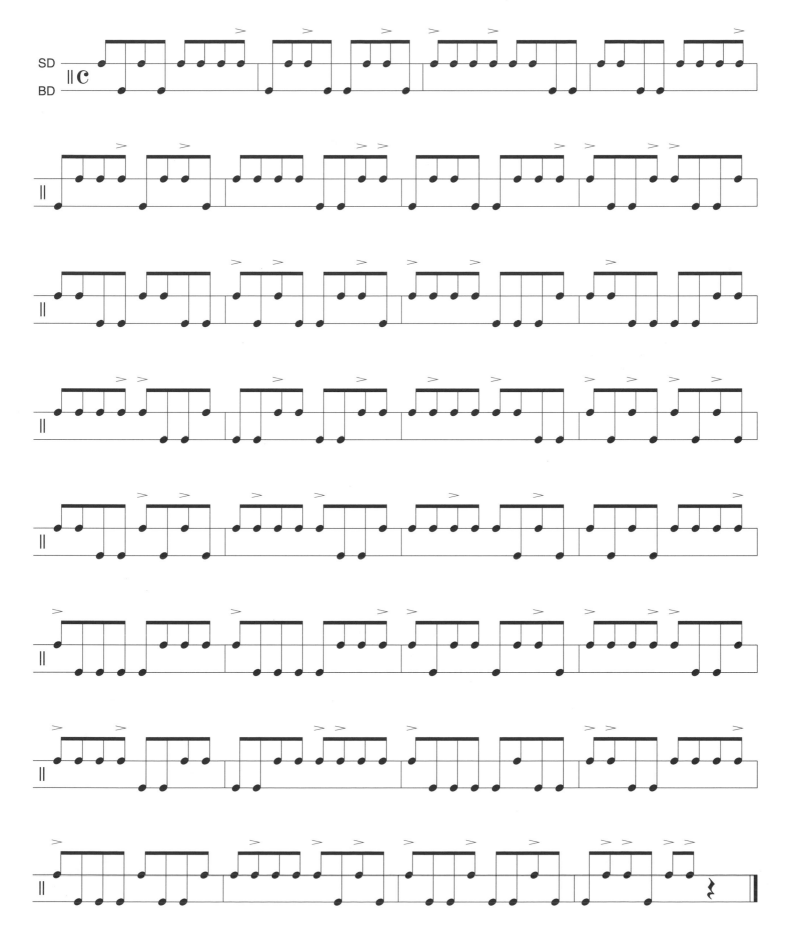

Section 2

Part 1: Triplet Speed And Endurance Exercise

The purpose of Part 1 is to help you develop a greater degree of bass drum speed and endurance. Using triplets, and starting at a comfortable tempo, play as many measures of triplets as you can. Do not push to the point of cramping or burning. Stop when you can no longer control a full measure of triplets.

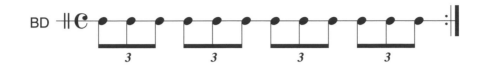

On the Endurance Progress Chart below, you can keep a record of your progress on a daily or weekly basis in the Date column.

Start at a comfortable tempo and write that tempo down under the M.M. (metronome marking) column.

As you play each measure of triplets, count out the total number of measures you are able to play without stopping, and mark it down in the Measures column.

The idea is to gradually increase both the speed (M.M.) and the number of measures you can play at that speed with each practice session. At the onset, *do not* attempt to play at a tempo faster than you're capable of playing. *Do not* attempt to play more measures than you can comfortably play. Foot speed, endurance, and control come with relaxed muscle action and gradual, consistent practice.

ENDURANCE PROGRESS CHART

Date	M.M.	# Of Measures

Part 2: Triplets With Accents

We'll now be playing the bass drum in triplets with accents added. Be sure to play the accented notes stronger than the non-accented ones. Note that the amount of accents per bar increases from one to six, so take your time. Repeat each pattern ten to twenty times, use a metronome, and increase the tempo gradually as you gain facility with these triplet accents.

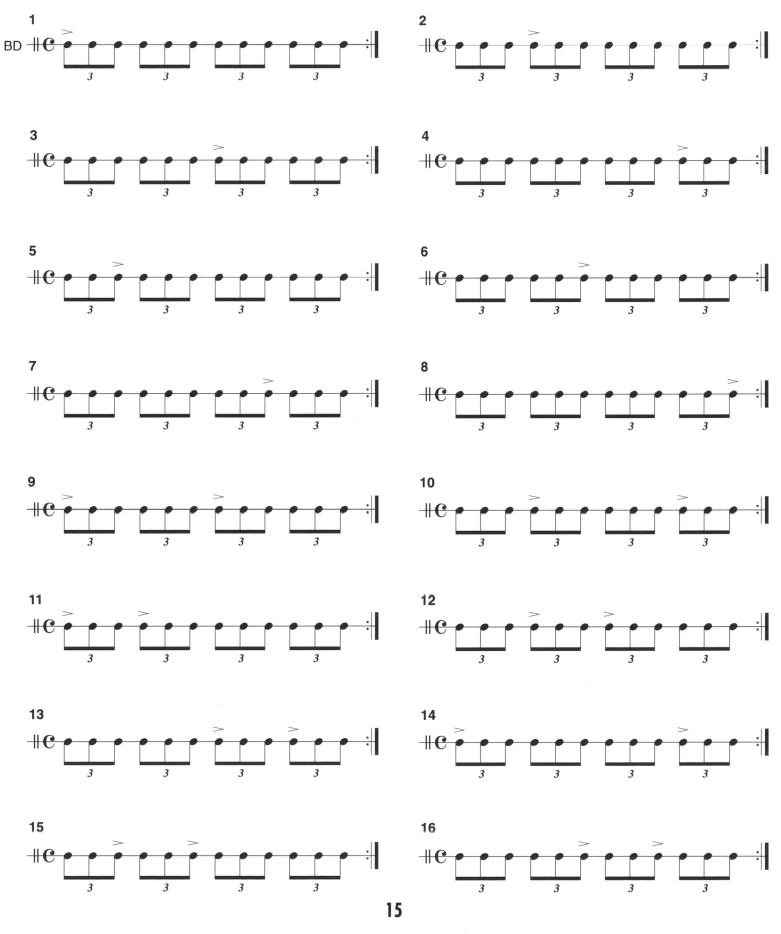

17

BD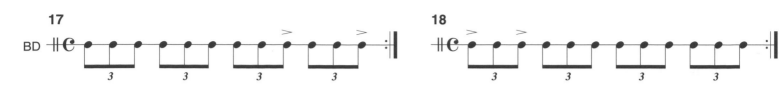

18

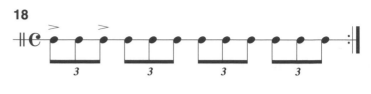

19

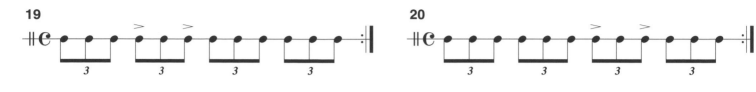

20

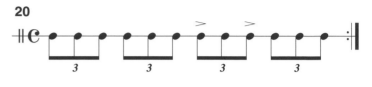

21

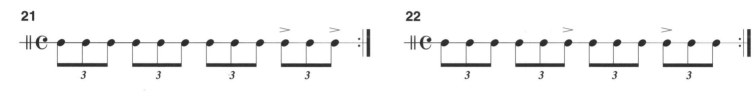

22

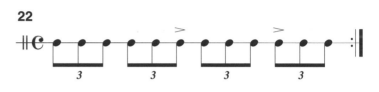

23

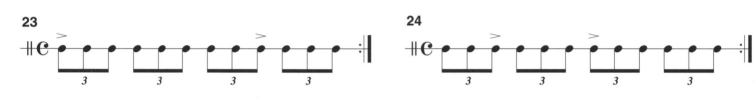

24

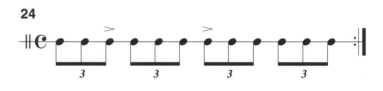

25

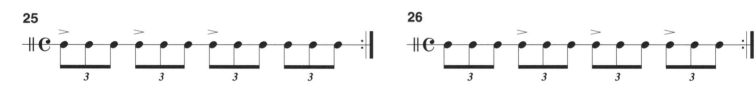

26

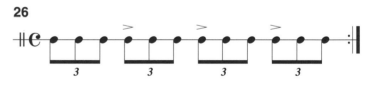

27

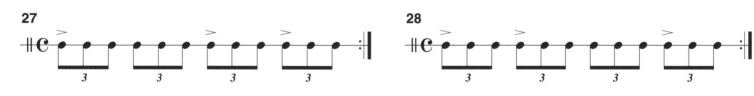

28

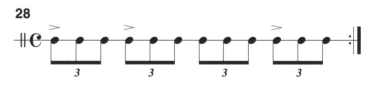

29

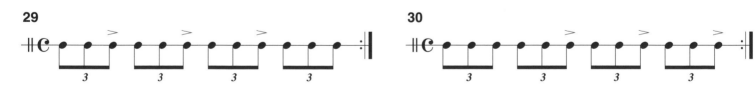

30

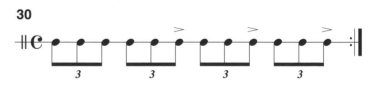

31

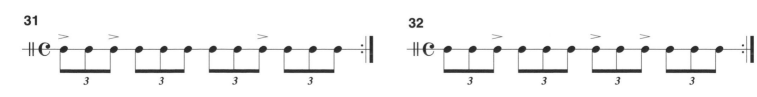

32

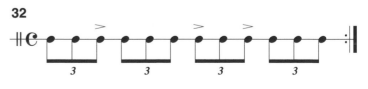

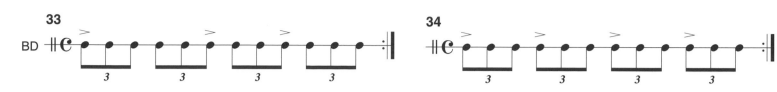
33

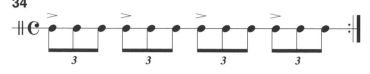
34

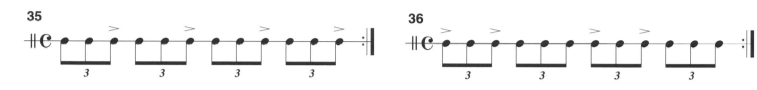
35

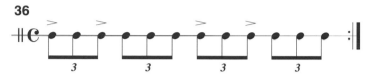
36

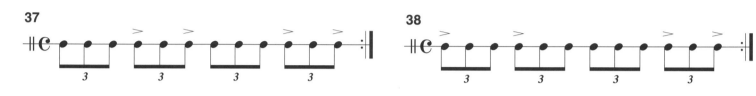
37

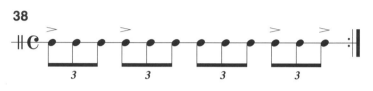
38

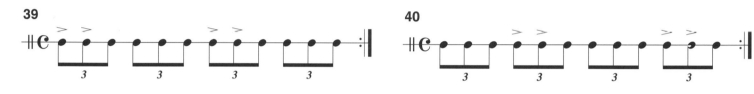
39

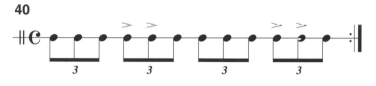
40

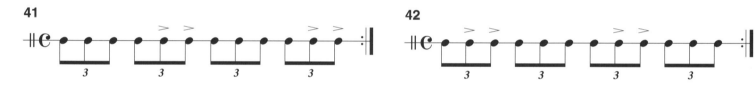
41

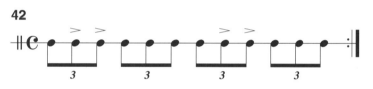
42

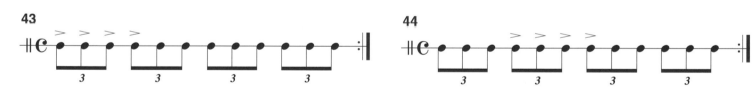
43

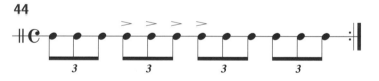
44

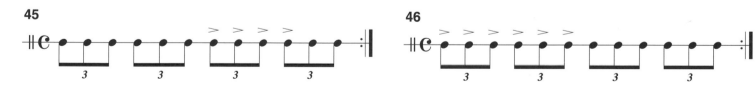
45

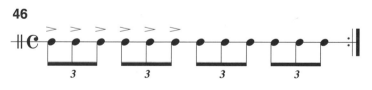
46

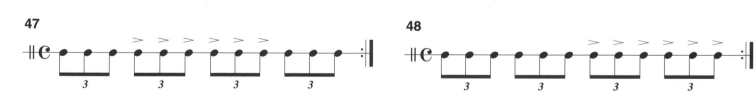
47

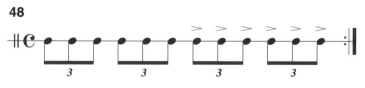
48

17

Part 3: Triplet Bass Drum Solo

Here is a bass drum solo using triplets, 8th notes, and quarter notes. Be sure the accents are accurately placed. Take your time, and strive for precise execution and control.

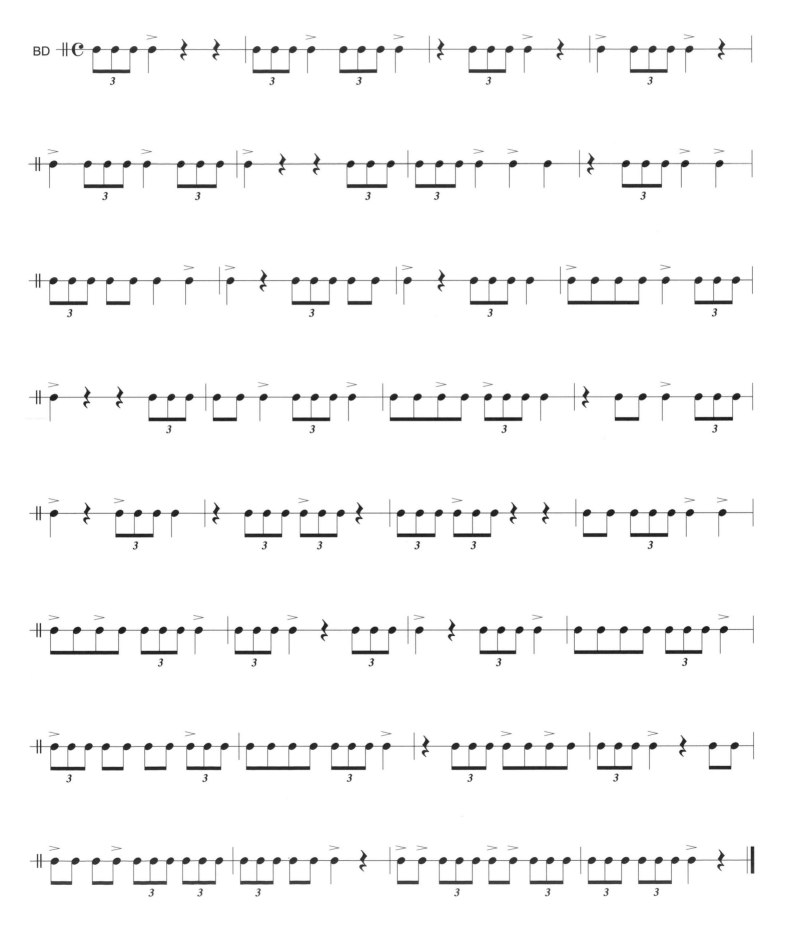

Part 4: Triplet Hand And Foot Patterns

The sixty-four exercises that follow utilize hand and foot patterns in 8th-note triplets. Repeat each pattern at least ten to twenty times. Set your metronome at a comfortable speed, and increase gradually with each new practice session. The emphasis on the bass drum gets greater as you work your way through the exercises, so take your time. Also, try moving the hand part to various components of the kit after you've mastered the pattern.

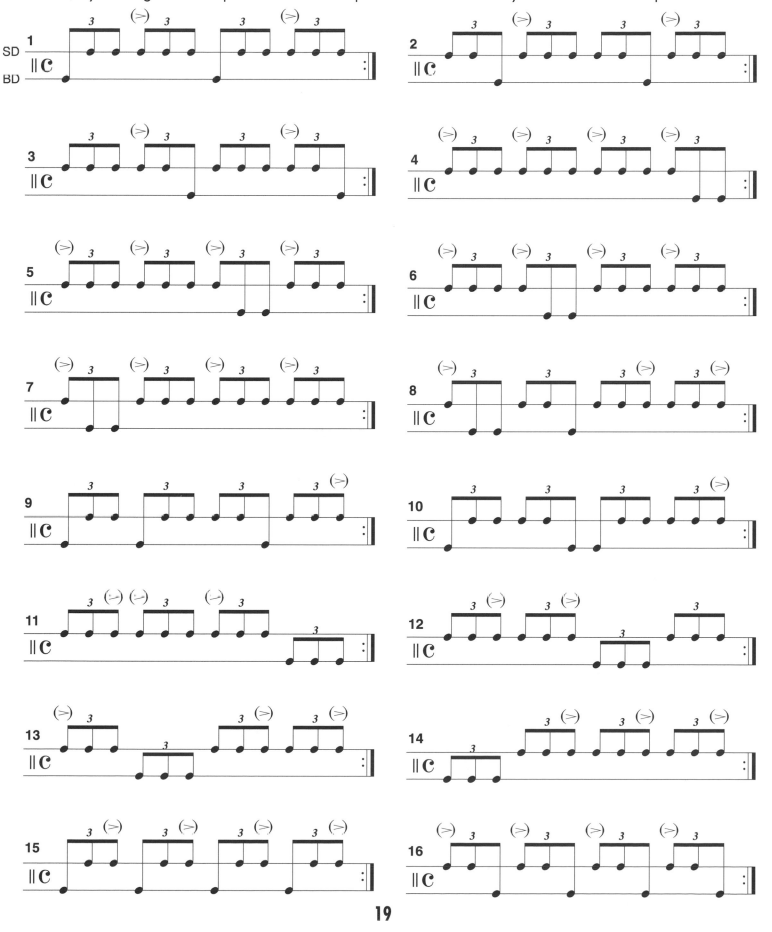

19

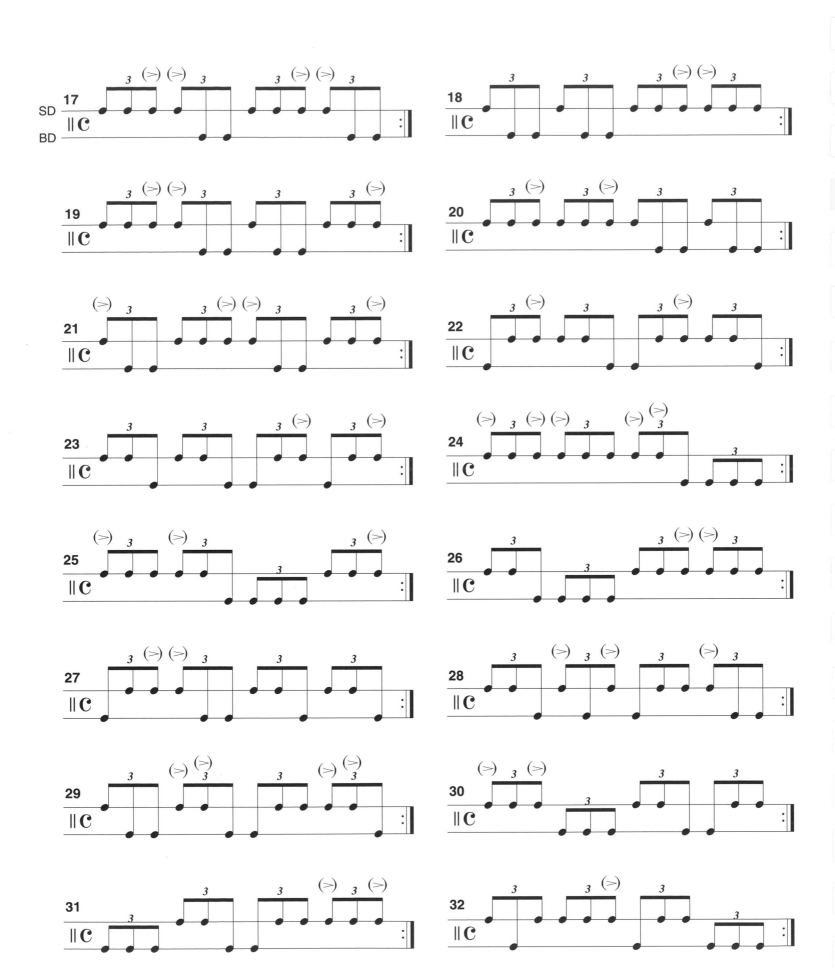

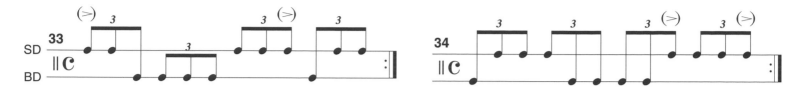
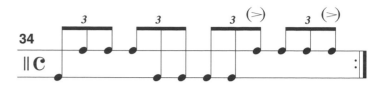
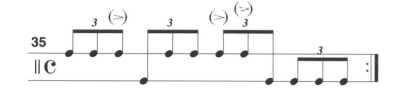
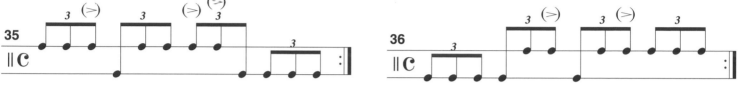
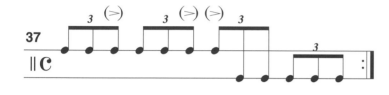
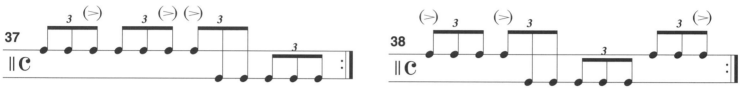
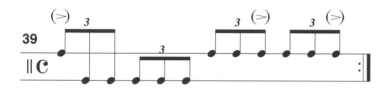
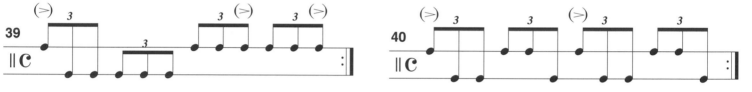
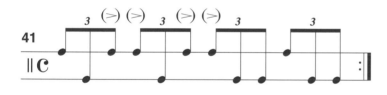
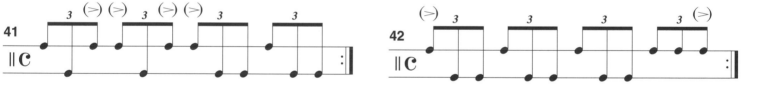
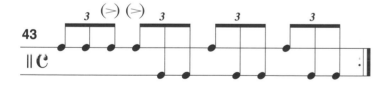
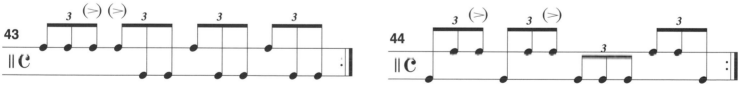
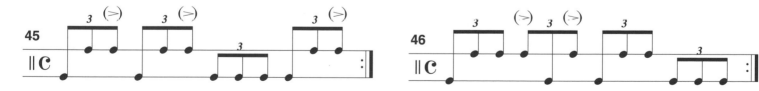
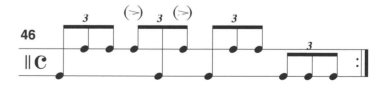
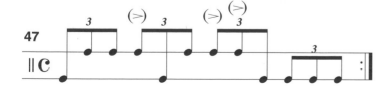
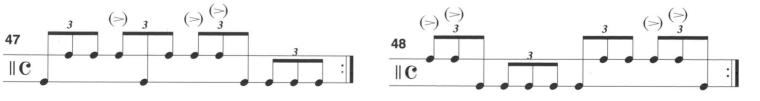

21

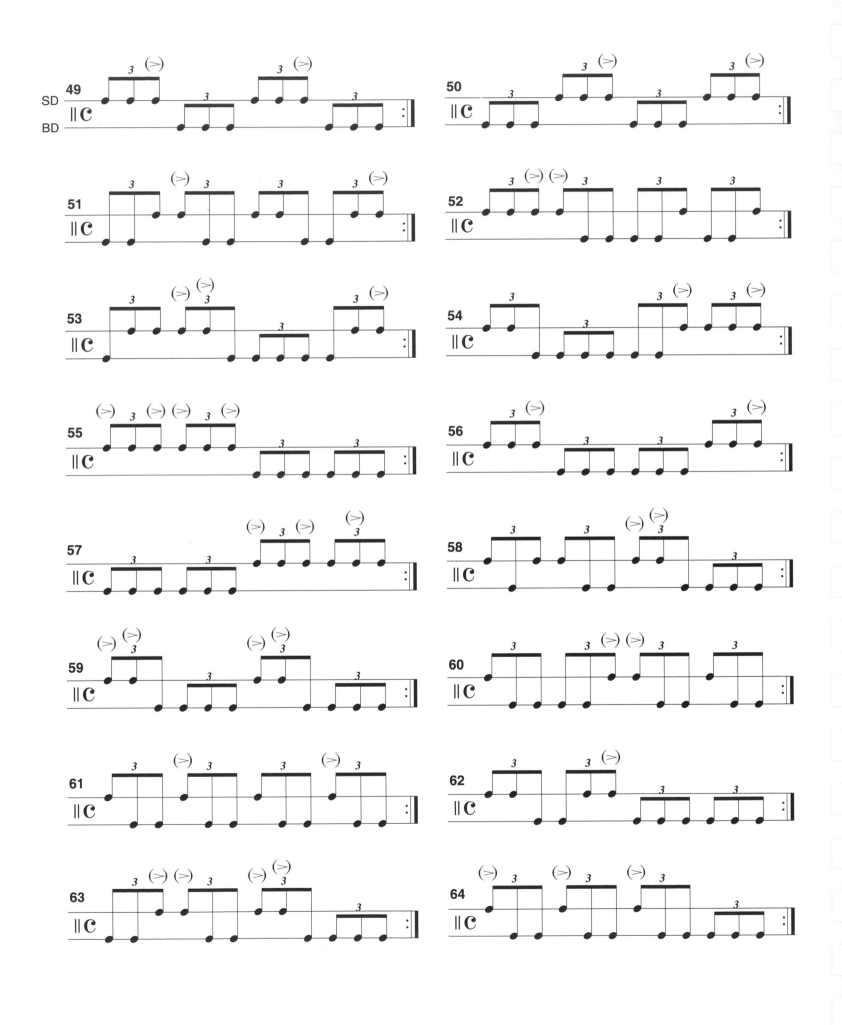

Part 5: Triplet Hand And Foot Solo

Here's a thirty-two-bar solo using most of the triplet hand and foot patterns presented on the previous pages, with accents added. Increase the tempo only after you've become familiar with the material. Your ultimate goal should be to play this solo from beginning to end without stopping and without any errors.

Section 3

Part 1: 16th-Note Figure 1 Speed And Endurance Exercise

The purpose of Part 1 is to help you develop a greater degree of bass drum speed and endurance. Using 16th-Note Figure 1, and starting at a comfortable tempo, play as many measures of the figure as you can. Do not push to the point of cramping or burning. Stop when you can no longer control a full measure of the figure.

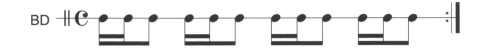

On the Endurance Progress Chart below, you can keep a record of your progress on a daily or weekly basis in the Date column.

Start at a comfortable tempo and write that tempo down under the M.M. (metronome marking) column.

As you play each measure of the 16th-note figure, count out the total number of measures you are able to play without stopping, and mark it down in the Measures column.

The idea is to gradually increase both the speed (M.M.) and the number of measures you can play at that speed with each practice session. At the onset, *do not* attempt to play at a tempo faster than you can comfortably play. *Do not* attempt to play more measures than you can comfortably play. Foot speed, endurance, and control come with relaxed muscle action and gradual, consistent practice.

ENDURANCE PROGRESS CHART

Date	M.M.	# Of Measures

Part 2: 16th-Note Figure 1 With Accents

Now that you've developed some endurance with 16th-Note Figure 1, it's time to work on adding accents to the repetitive figure. Make a clear distinction between the accented and non-accented notes, and repeat each exercise five to ten times without stopping.

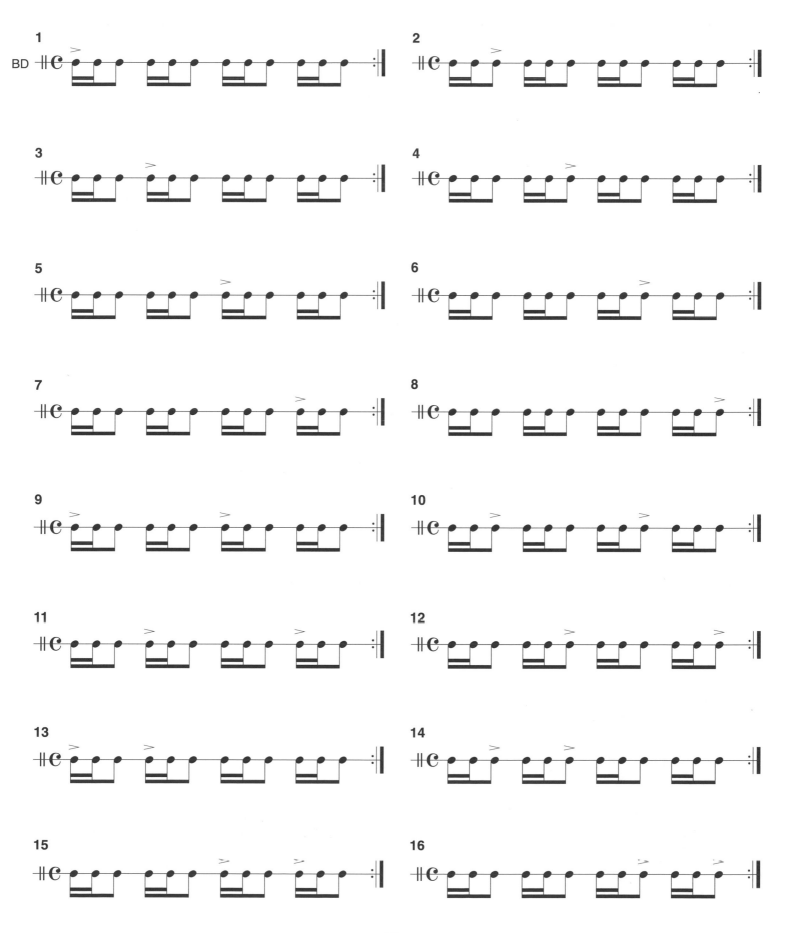

17

BD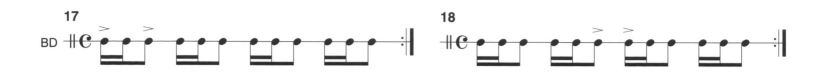

18

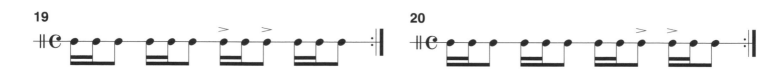

19

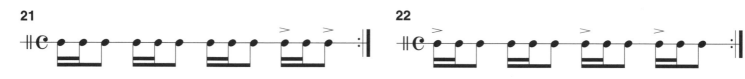

20

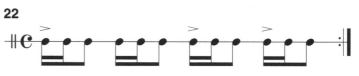

21

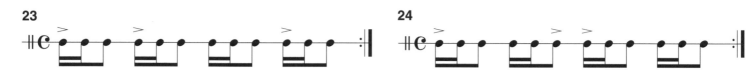

22

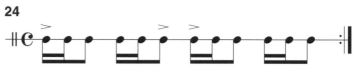

23

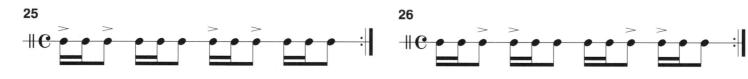

24

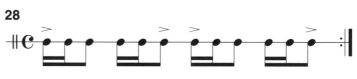

25

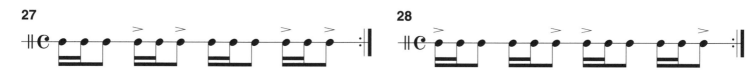

26

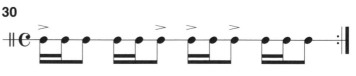

27

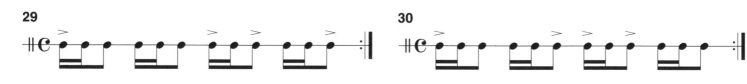

28

29

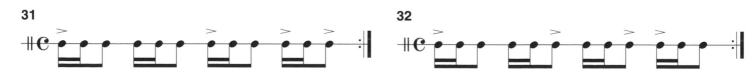

30

31

32

33

BD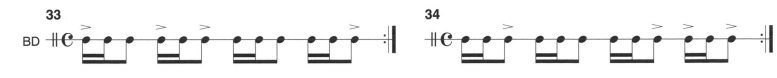

34

35

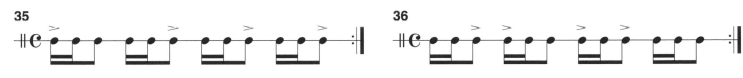

36

37

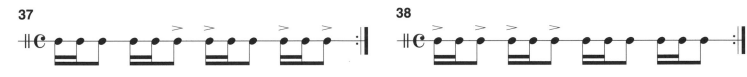

38

39

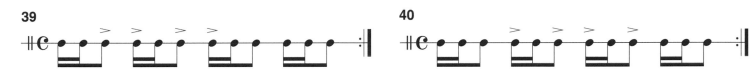

40

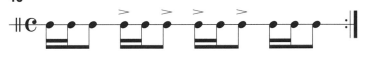

41

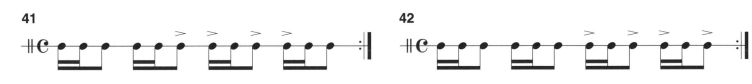

42

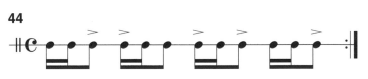

43

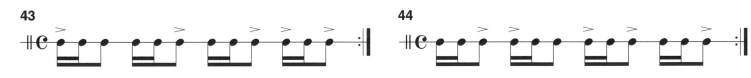

44

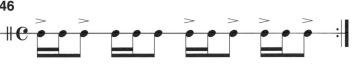

45

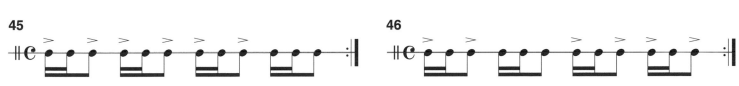

46

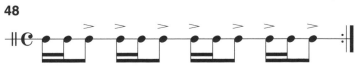

47

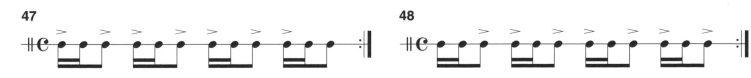

48

Part 3: 16th-Note Figure 1 Bass Drum Solo

The thirty-two-bar solo below uses 16th-Note Figure 1 with 8th notes and quarter notes. Considerable stress is placed on the foot during the latter part of the solo. Start at a comfortable tempo and increase gradually.

Part 4: 16th-Note Figure 1 Hand And Foot Patterns

Part 4 involves the use of 16th-Note Figure 1 in a series of hand and foot coordination patterns. Start out slowly, and repeat each pattern ten to twenty times. The demands on the bass drum foot increase as you progress further into Part 4.

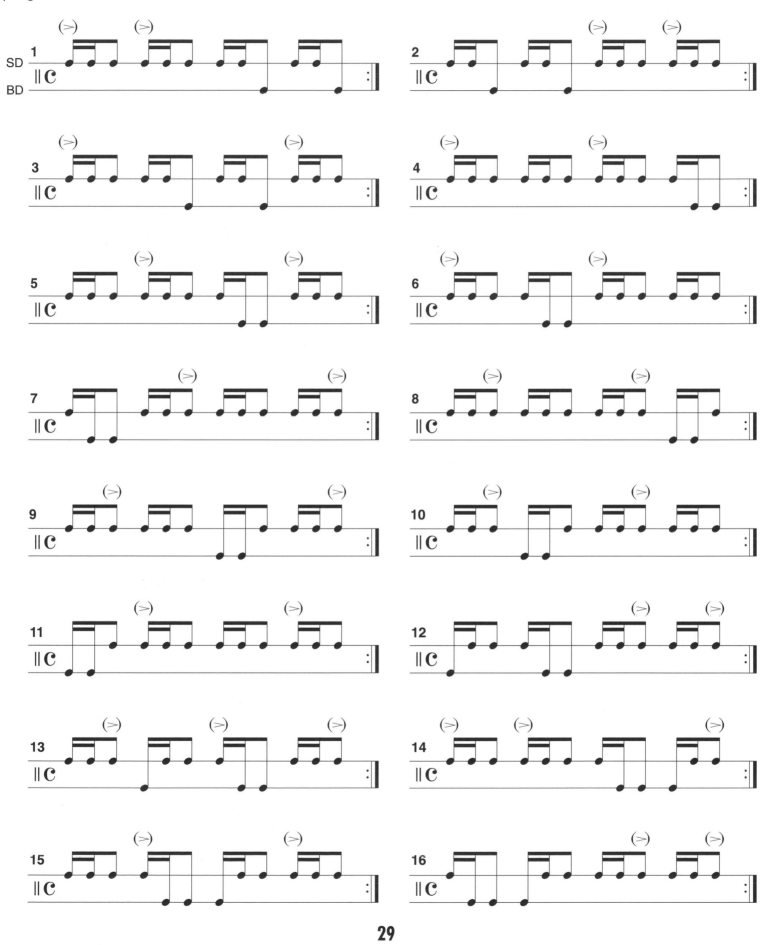

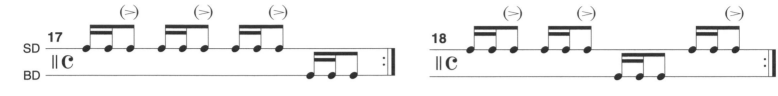

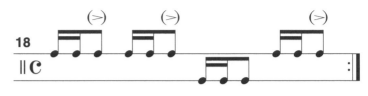

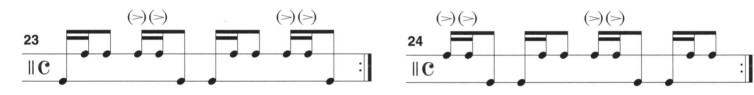

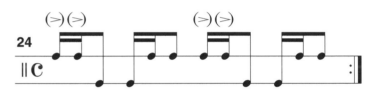

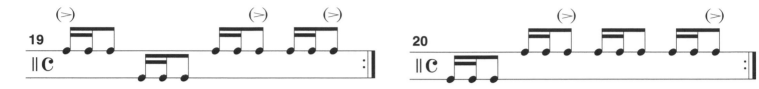

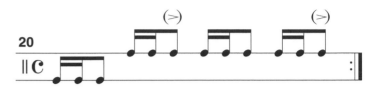

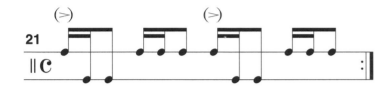

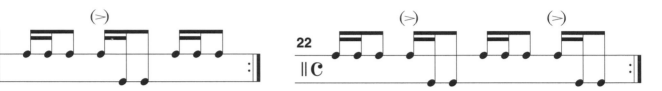

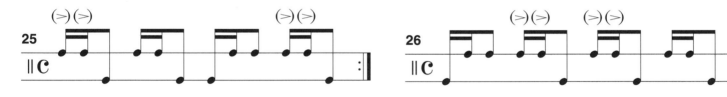

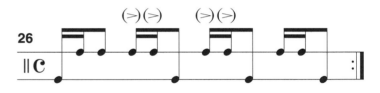

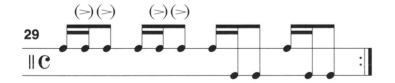

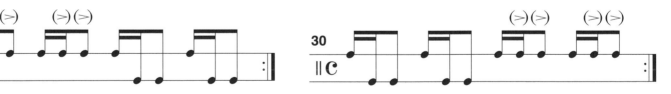

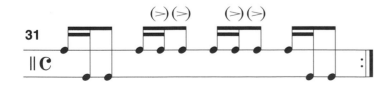

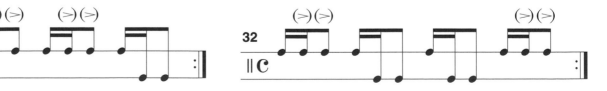

30

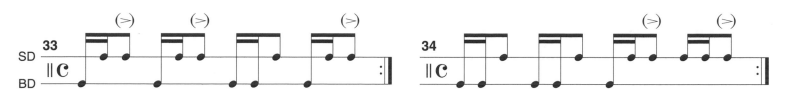

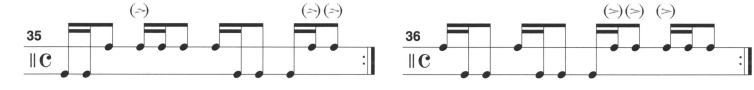

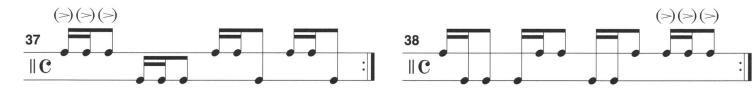

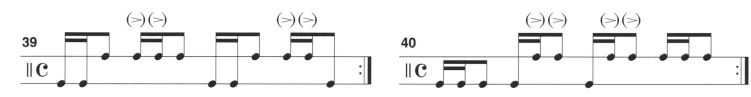

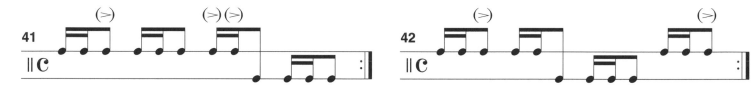

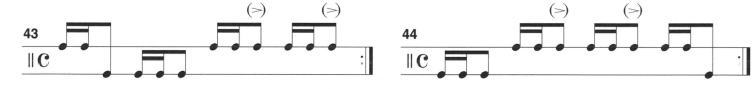

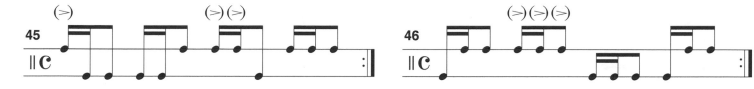

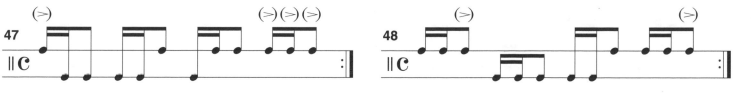

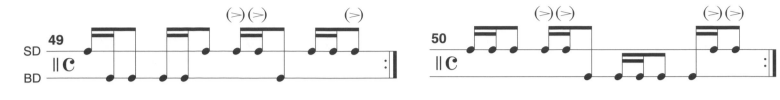

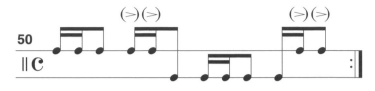

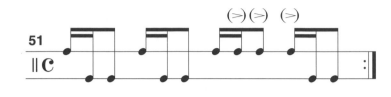

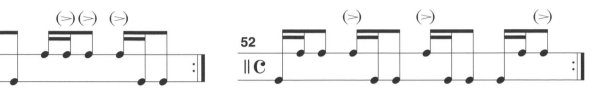

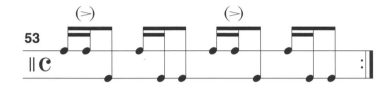

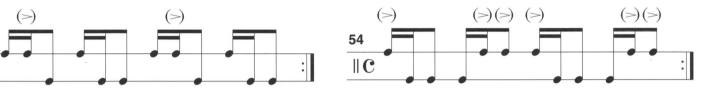

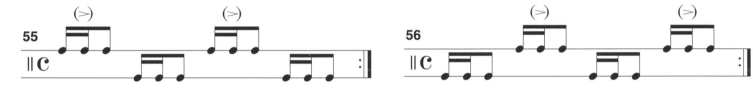

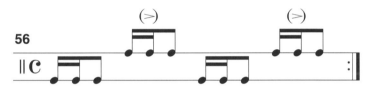

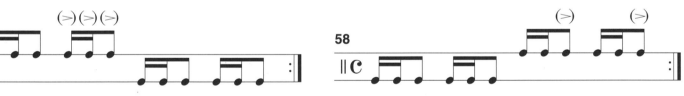

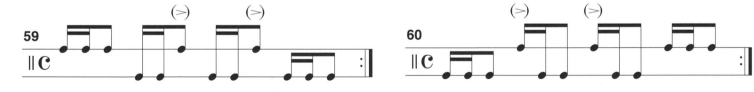

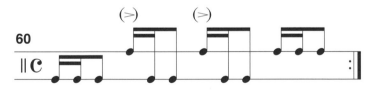

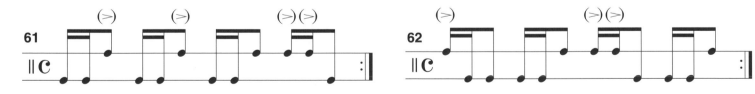

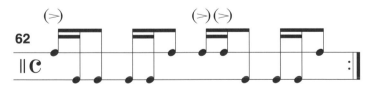

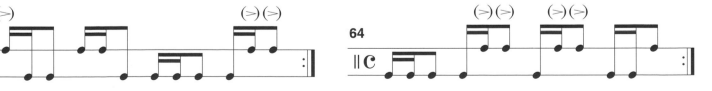

Part 5: 16th-Note Figure 1 Hand And Foot Solo

We'll now incorporate most of the previously studied hand and foot patterns into the following thirty-two-bar solo. Isolate any problem measures, then go back and try to play the solo from beginning to end without a mistake.

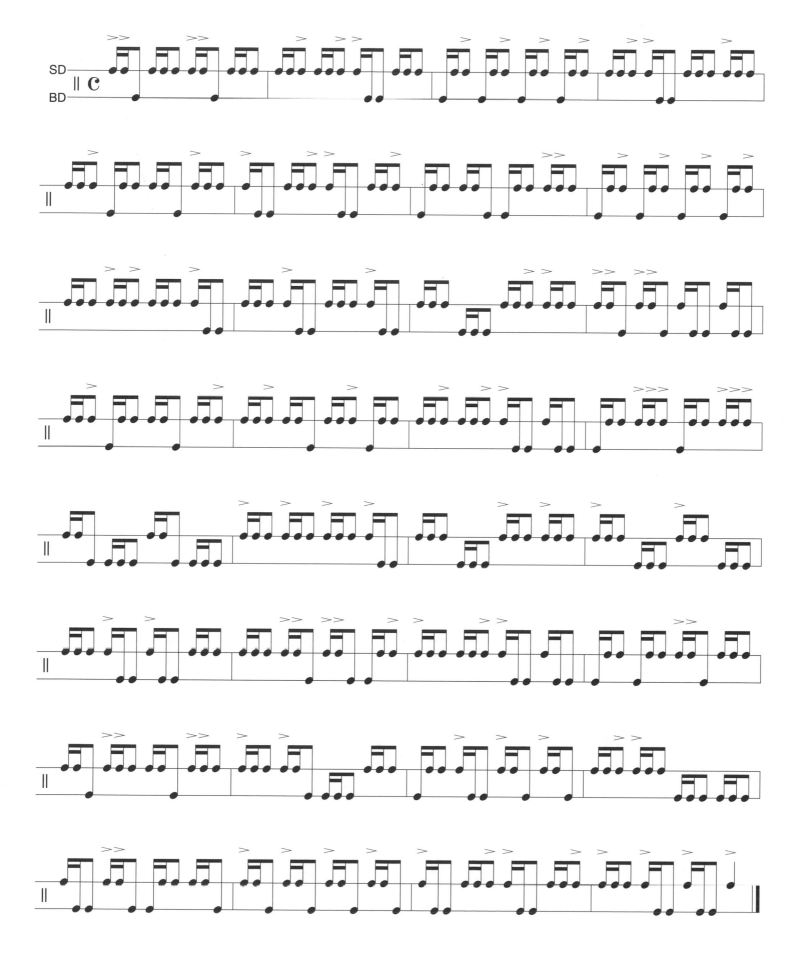

Section 4

Part 1: 16th-Note Figure 2 Speed And Endurance Exercise

The purpose of Part 1 is to help you develop a greater degree of bass drum speed and endurance. Using 16th-Note Figure 2, and starting at a comfortable tempo, play as many measures of the figure as you can. Do not push to the point of cramping or burning. Stop when you can no longer control a full measure of the figure.

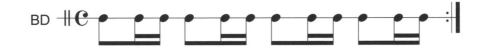

On the Endurance Progress Chart below, you can keep a record of your progress on a daily or weekly basis in the Date column.

Start at a comfortable tempo and write that tempo down under the M.M. (metronome marking) column.

As you play each measure of the 16th-note figure, count out the total number of measures you are able to play without stopping, and mark it down in the Measures column.

The idea is to gradually increase both the speed (M.M.), and the number of measures you can play at that speed, with each practice session. At the onset, *do not* attempt to play at a tempo faster than you're capable of playing. *Do not* attempt to play more measures than you can comfortably play. Foot speed, endurance, and control come with relaxed muscle action and gradual, consistent practice.

ENDURANCE PROGRESS CHART

Date	M.M.	# Of Measures

Part 2: 16th-Note Figure 2 With Accents

Applying accents to 16th-Note Figure 2 will also help you attain a greater level of foot control and strength. Take your time with these patterns, starting out slowly and gradually increasing the tempo over a period of time. Repeat each exercise five to ten times before moving on to the next one, and practice them heel up and heel down.

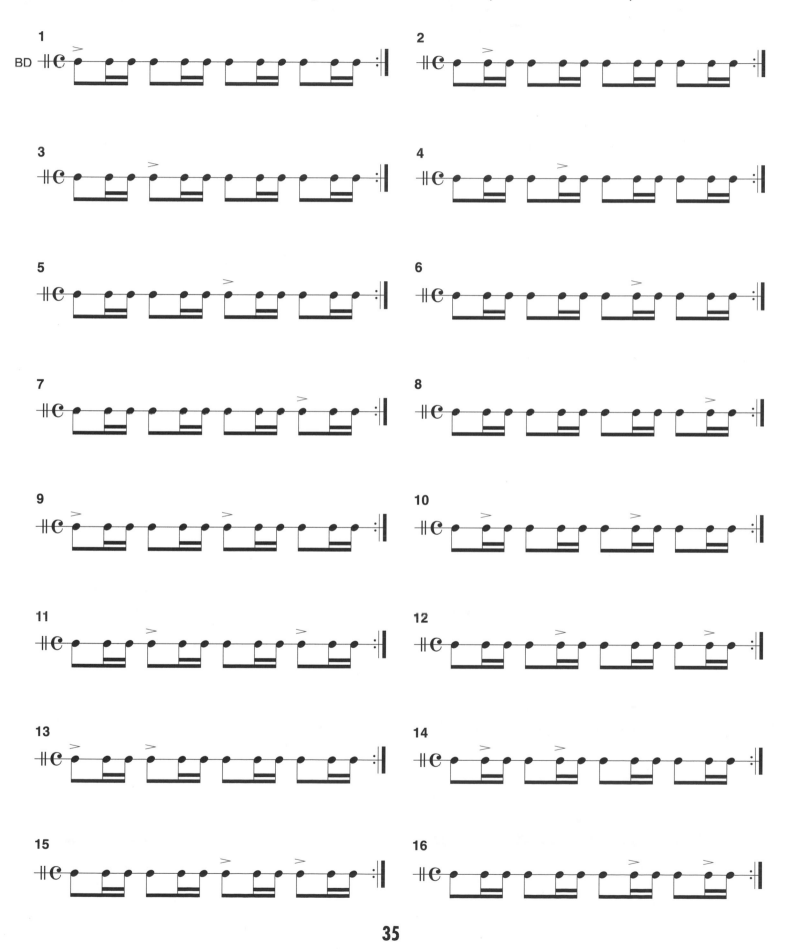

17

BD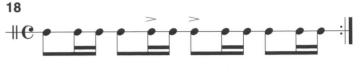

18

19

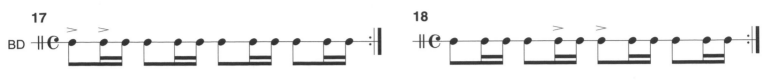

20

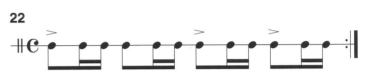

21

22

23

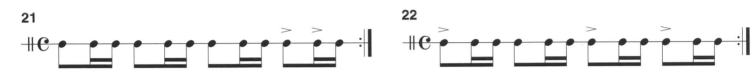

24

25

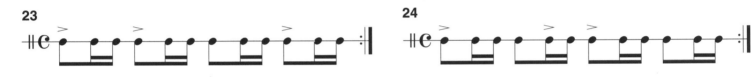

26

27

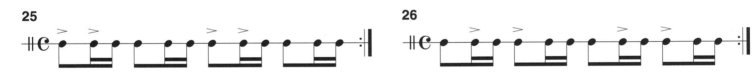

28

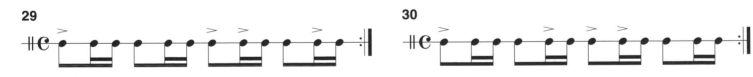

29

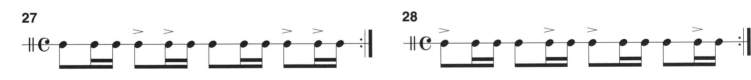

30

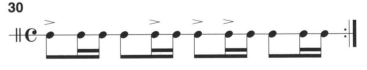

31

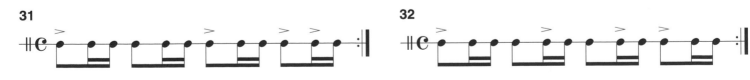

32

33

BD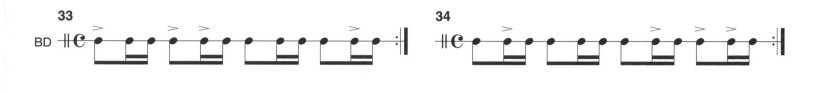

34

35

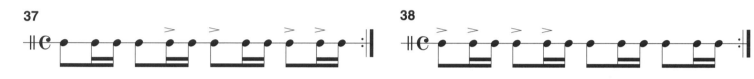

36

37

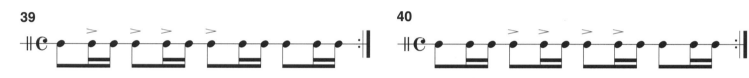

38

39

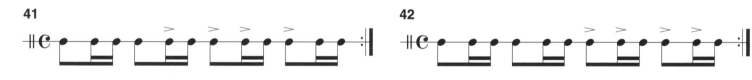

40

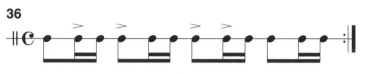

41

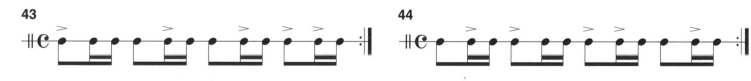

42

43

44

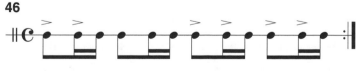

45

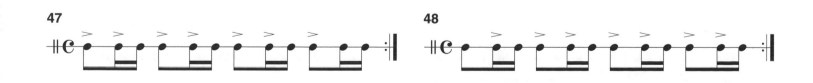

46

47

48

Part 3: 16th-Note Figure 2 Bass Drum Solo

Here's a bass drum solo utilizing 16th-note rhythmic Figure 2. Strive for precise execution, and remember to use a metronome or drum machine to assure a steady, even time flow.

Part 4: 16th-Note Figure 2 Hand And Foot Patterns

Here's another series of hand and foot patterns, this time using 16th-Note Figure 2. Practice the exercises heel up and heel down. After you've mastered each pattern, try moving the hand part around to the various parts of the kit in a random fashion. The accents, indicated in parentheses, are optional.

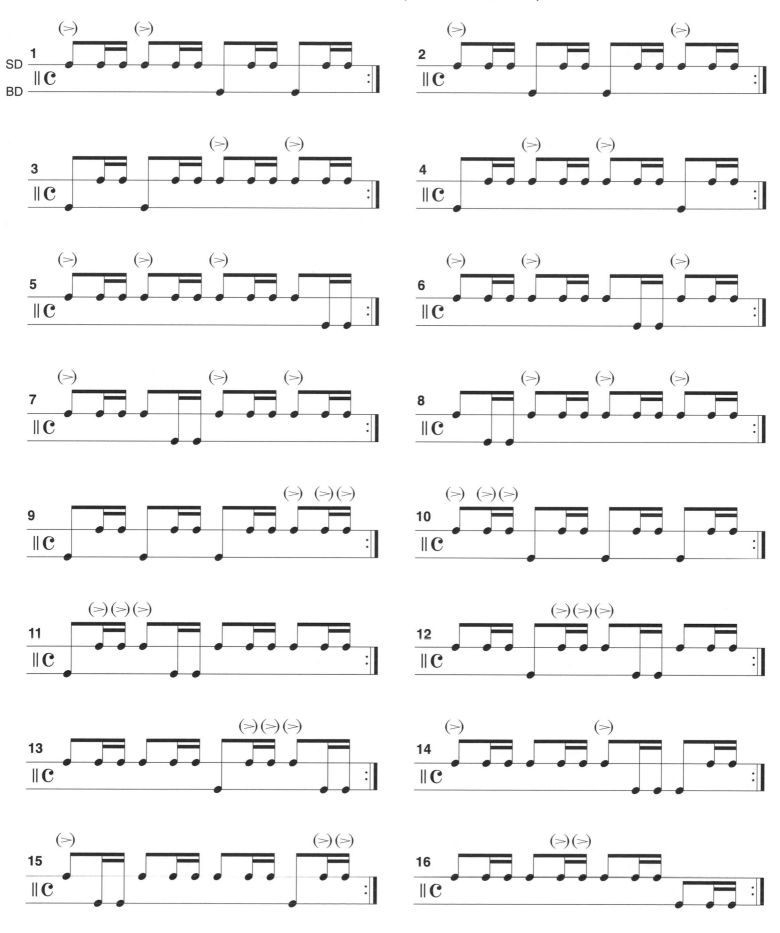

39

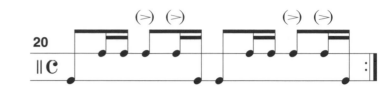

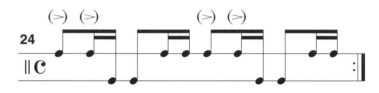

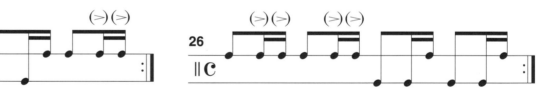

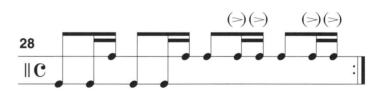

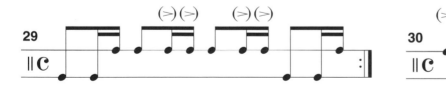

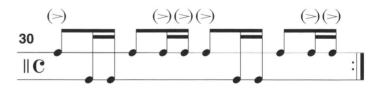

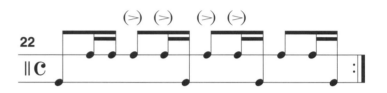

40

SD

BD

33

34

35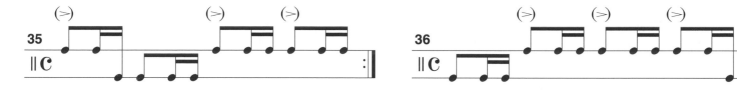

36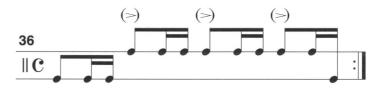

37

38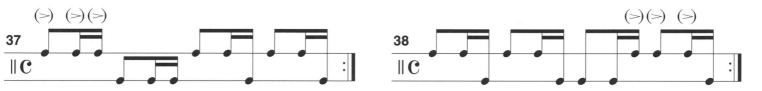

39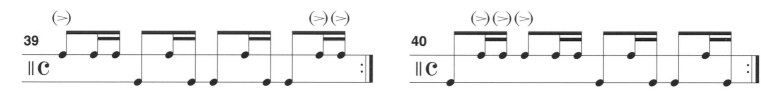

40

41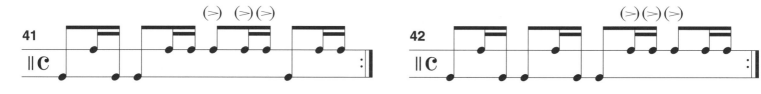

42

43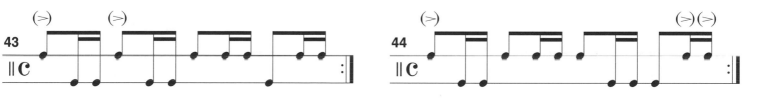

44

45

46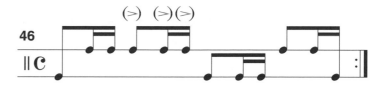

47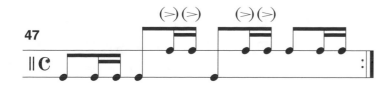

48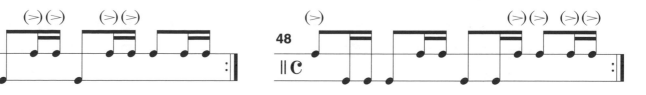

41

SD

BD

49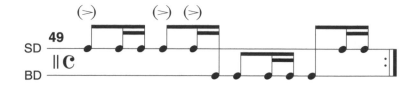

50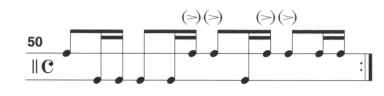

51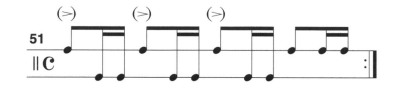

52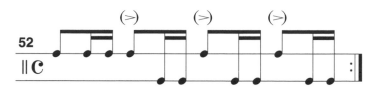

53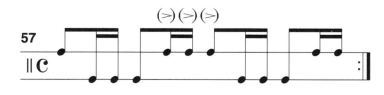

54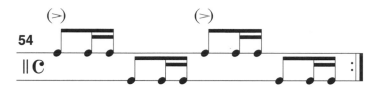

55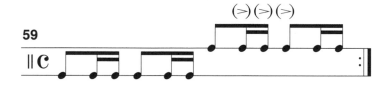

56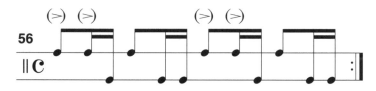

57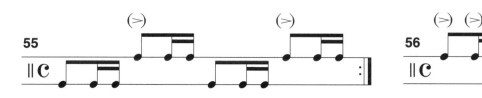

58

59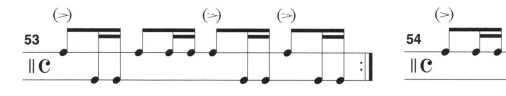

60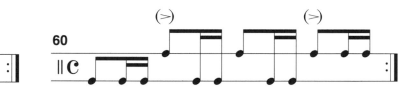

61

62

63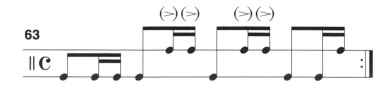

64

Part 5: 16th-Note Figure 2 Hand And Foot Solo

Practice this solo slowly at first, increasing the speed as you become more familiar with the material. Watch the accents, and be certain they're placed accurately. Use a metronome, and practice both heel up and heel down.

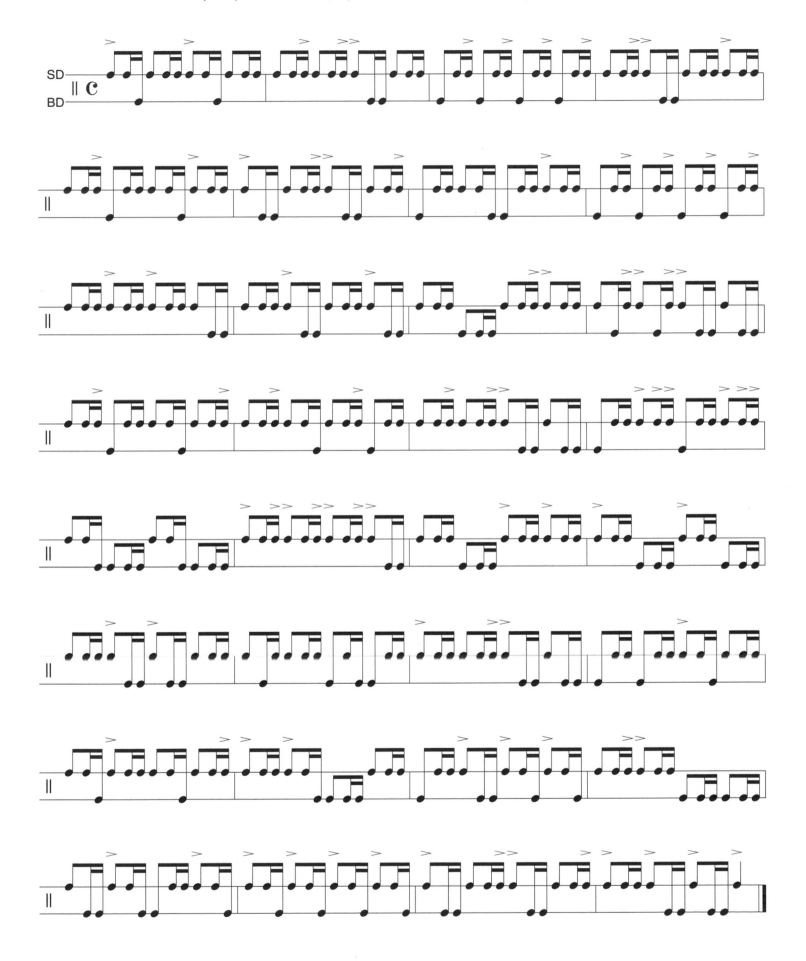

Section 5

Part 1: 16th-Note Speed And Endurance Exercise

The purpose of Part 1 is to help you develop a greater degree of bass drum speed and endurance. Using 16th notes, and starting at a comfortable tempo, play as many measures of 16th notes as you can. Do not push to the point of cramping or burning. Stop when you can no longer control a full measure of 16th notes.

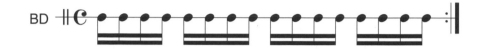

On the Endurance Progress Chart below, you can keep a record of your progress on a daily or weekly basis in the Date column.

Start at a comfortable tempo and write that tempo down under the M.M. (metronome marking) column.

As you play each measure of 16th notes, count out the total number of measures you are able to play without stopping, and mark it down in the Measures column.

The idea is to gradually increase both the speed (M.M.), and the number of measures you can play at that speed with each practice session. At the onset, *do not* attempt to play at a tempo faster than you're capable of playing. *Do not* attempt to play more measures than you can comfortably play. Foot speed, endurance, and control come with relaxed muscle action and gradual, consistent practice.

ENDURANCE PROGRESS CHART

Date	M.M.	# Of Measures

Part 2: 16th Notes With Accents

Part 2 involves the use of 16th notes with accents. Set your metronome at a comfortable speed for starters, increasing gradually with each practice session. Sixteenth notes place a greater demand on foot strength and endurance, so take your time. Rest at regular intervals, and resume after your leg muscles have had a chance to rest. Repeat each pattern ten to twenty times without stopping.

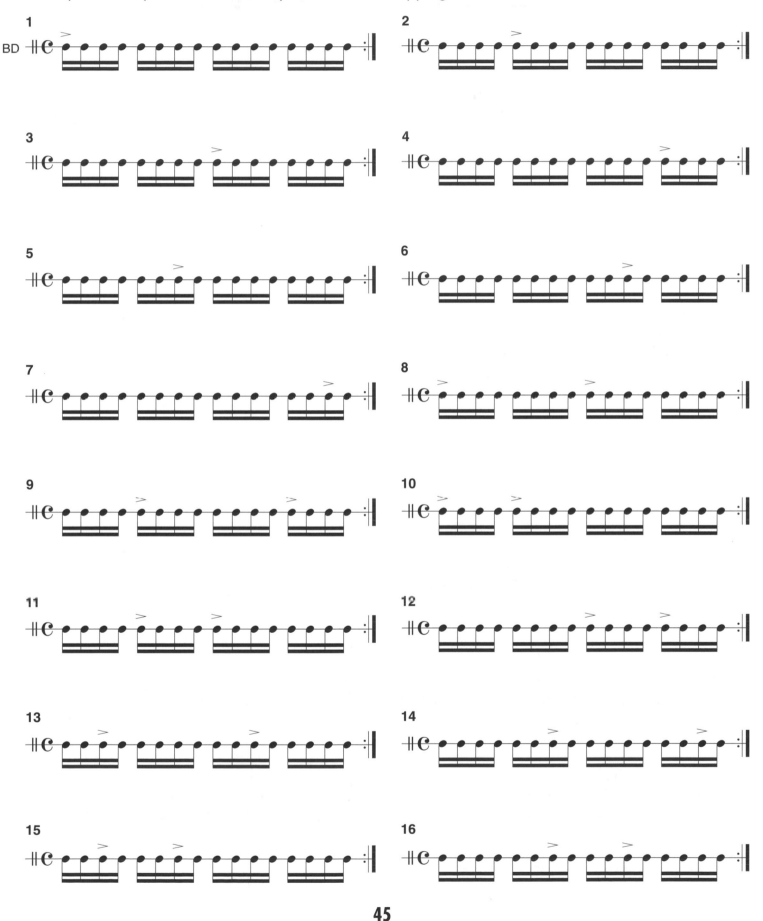

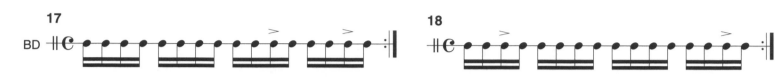

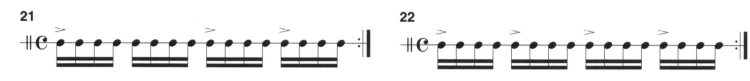

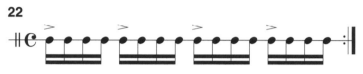

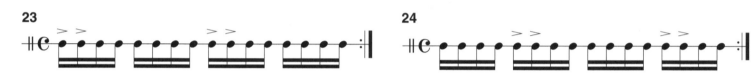

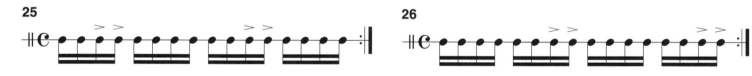

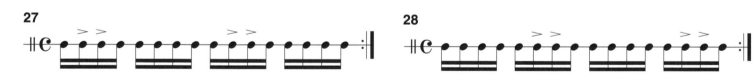

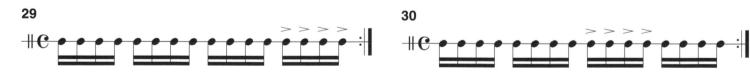

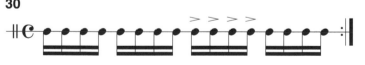

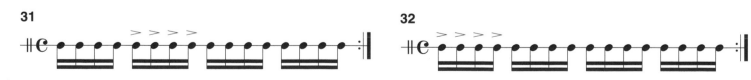

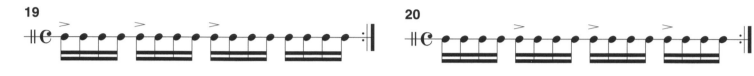

33

BD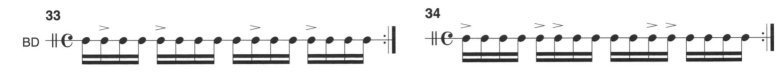

34

35

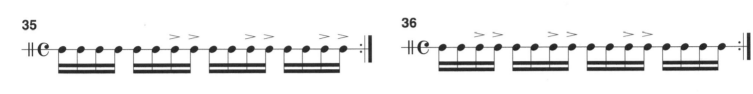

36

37

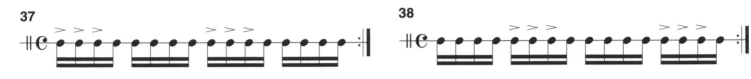

38

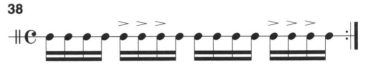

39

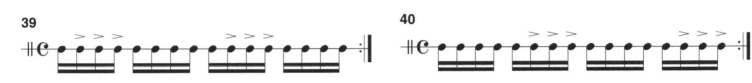

40

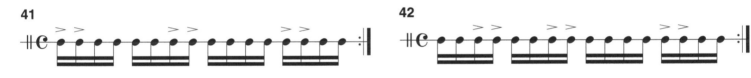

41

42

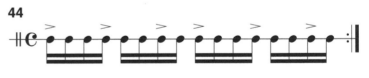

43

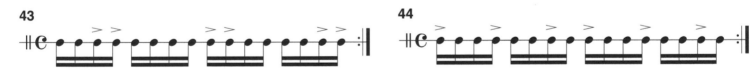

44

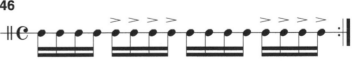

45

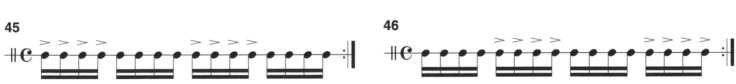

46

47

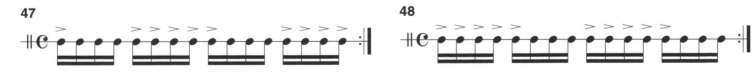

48

Part 3: 16th-Note Bass Drum Solo

This bass drum solo uses 16th notes, 8th notes, and quarter notes. Be sure to play all of the accented notes much stronger than the non-accented notes. Try to play the solo from beginning to end at a comfortable tempo and without a mistake.

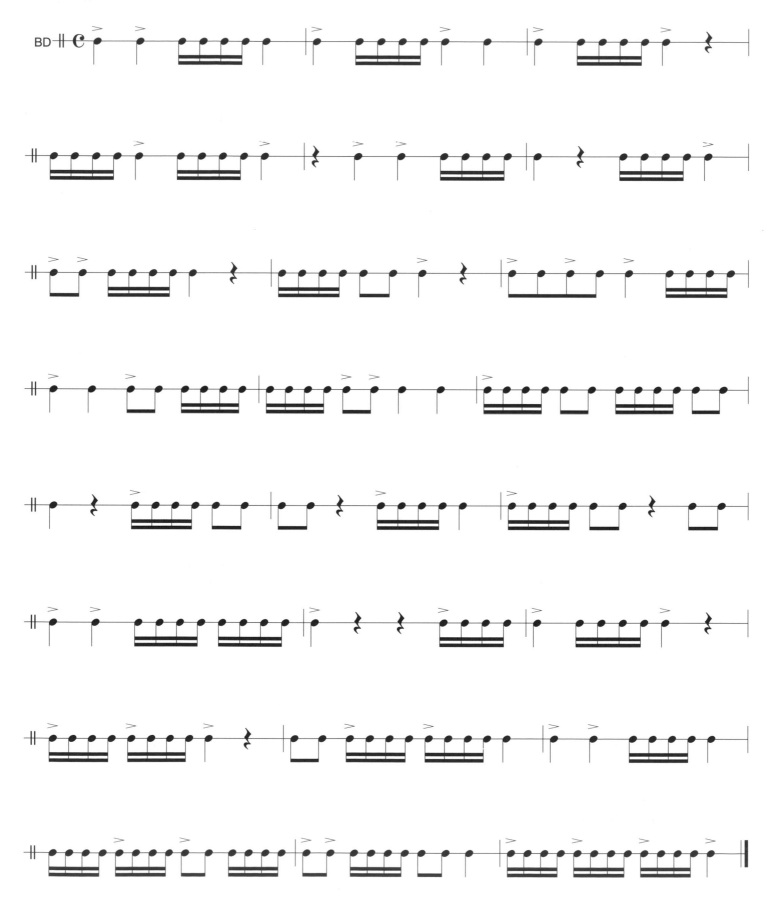

48

Part 4: 16th-Note Hand And Foot Patterns

We'll now move on to hand and foot patterns using 16th-note combinations. Stronger emphasis is gradually placed on the foot as the number of bass drum notes per bar increases from two to twelve. Try them using both heel up *and* heel down, and start out very slowly.

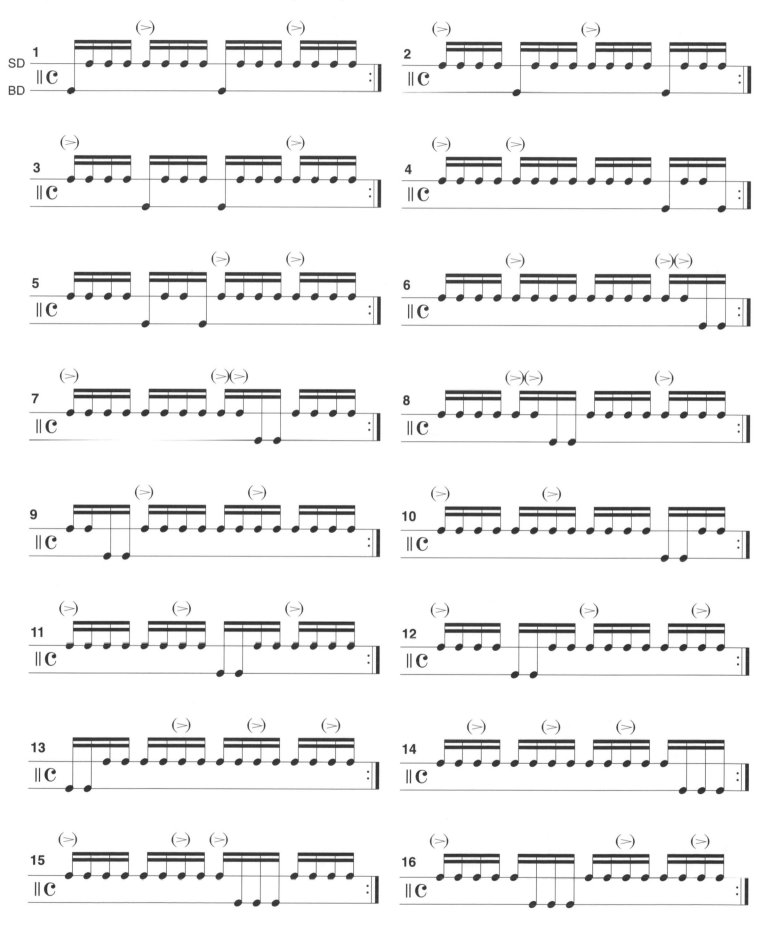

49

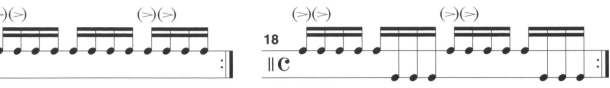

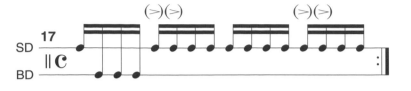

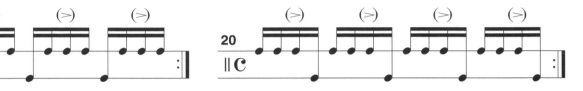

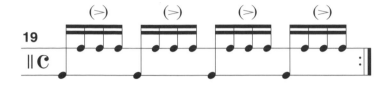

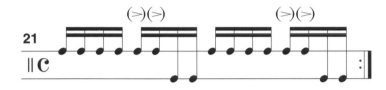

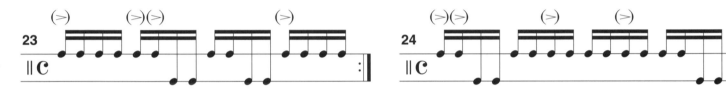

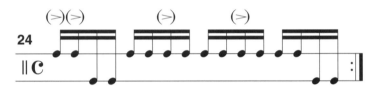

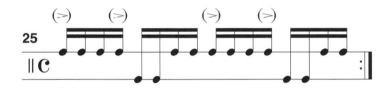

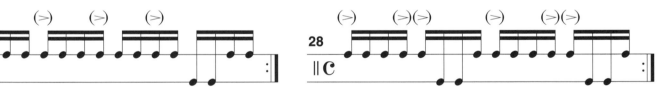

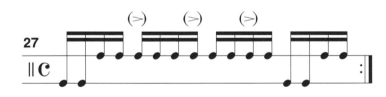

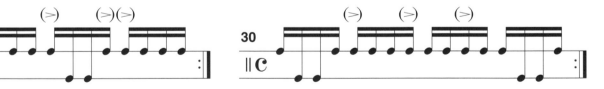

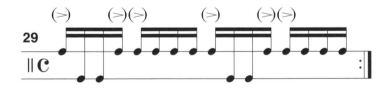

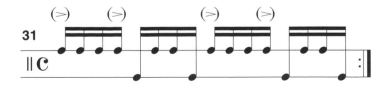

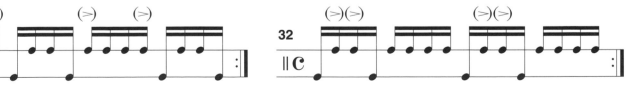

50

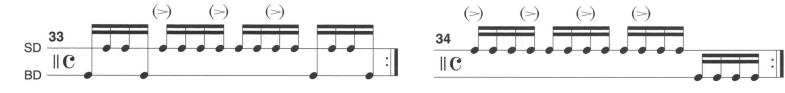

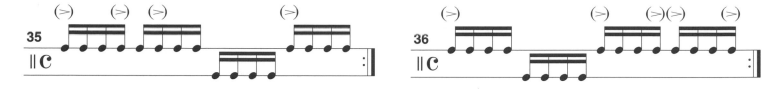

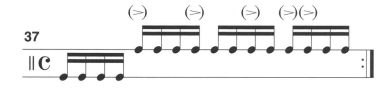

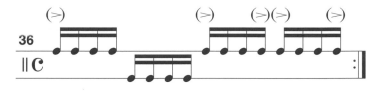

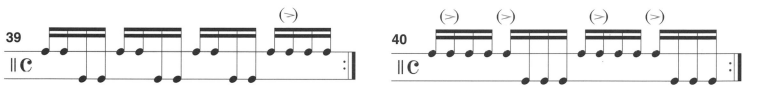

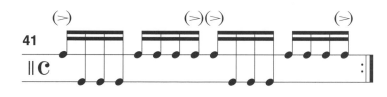

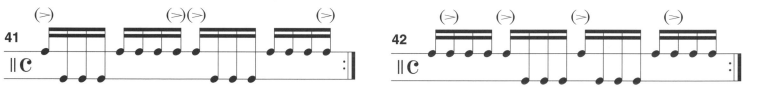

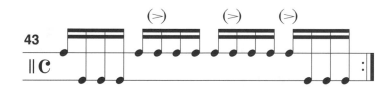

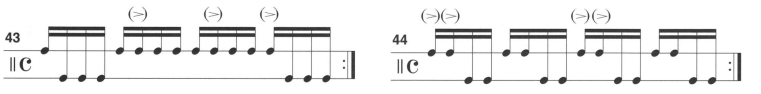

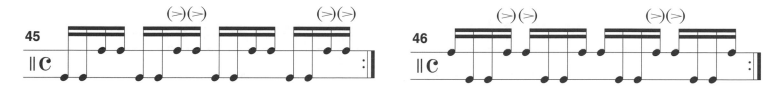

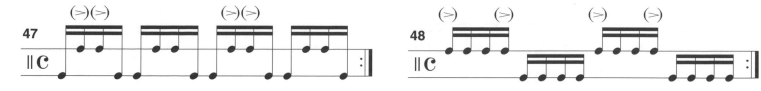

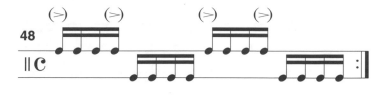

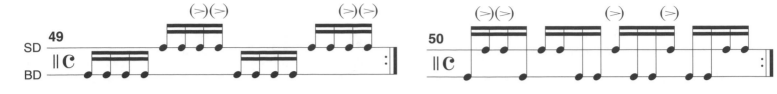

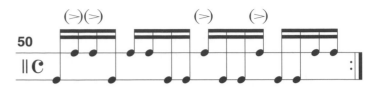

SD
BD

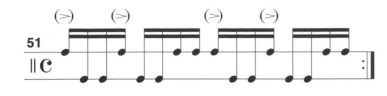

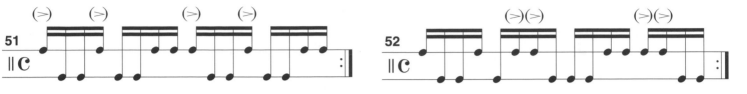

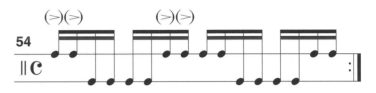

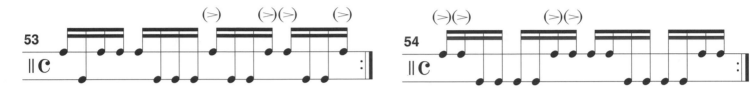

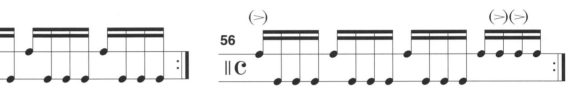

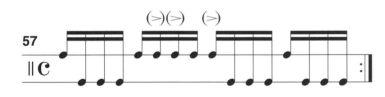

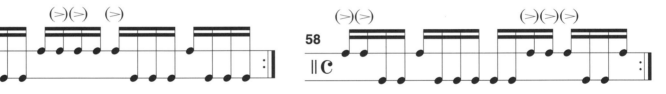

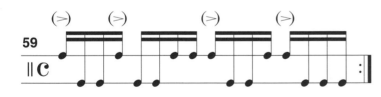

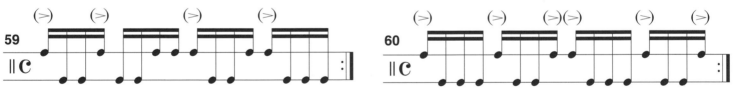

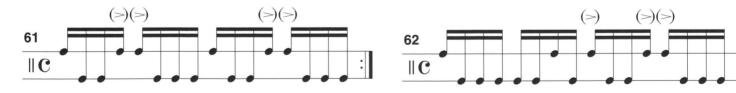

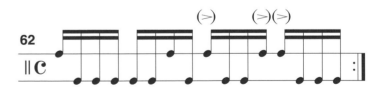

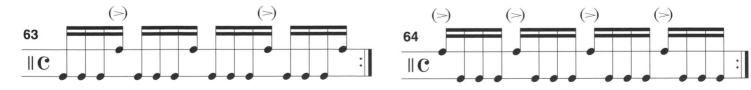

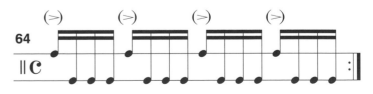

52

Part 5: 16th-Note Hand And Foot Solo

Here's a twenty-four-bar solo using most of the 16th-note hand and foot patterns studied on the previous pages. Also note the wide use of accents throughout the solo. Once again, the ultimate goal is to play the solo from beginning to end without stopping and without a mistake.

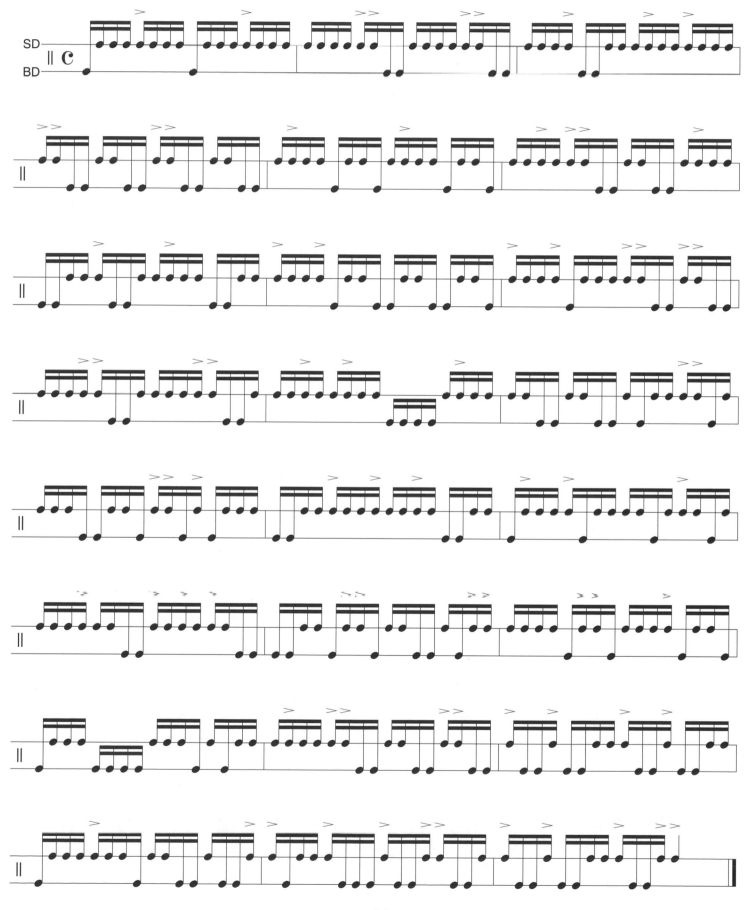

53

Section 6

Part 1: 16th-Note-Triplet Speed And Endurance Exercise

The purpose of Part 1 is to help you develop a greater degree of bass drum speed and endurance. Using 16th-note triplets, and starting at a comfortable tempo, play as many measures of 16th-note triplets as you can. Do not push to the point of cramping or burning. Stop when you can no longer control a full measure of 16th-note triplets.

On the Endurance Progress Chart below, you can keep a record of your progress on a daily or weekly basis in the Date column.

Start at a comfortable tempo and write that tempo down under the M.M. (metronome marking) column.

As you play each measure of 16th-note triplets, count out the total number of measures you are able to play without stopping, and mark it down in the Measures column.

The idea is to gradually increase both the speed (M.M.) and the number of measures you can play at that speed with each practice session. At the onset, *do not* attempt to play at a tempo faster than you're capable of playing. *Do not* attempt to play more measures than you can comfortably play. Foot speed, endurance, and control come with relaxed muscle action and gradual, consistent practice.

ENDURANCE PROGRESS CHART

Date	M.M.	# Of Measures

Part 2: 16th-Note Triplets With Accents

Sixteenth-note triplets with accents can present a considerable technical challenge. Don't be in a rush to increase your speed. Repeat each pattern five to ten times without stopping, and maintain a steady tempo through the use of a metronome or drum machine. Remember to practice these patterns with both heel up and heel down.

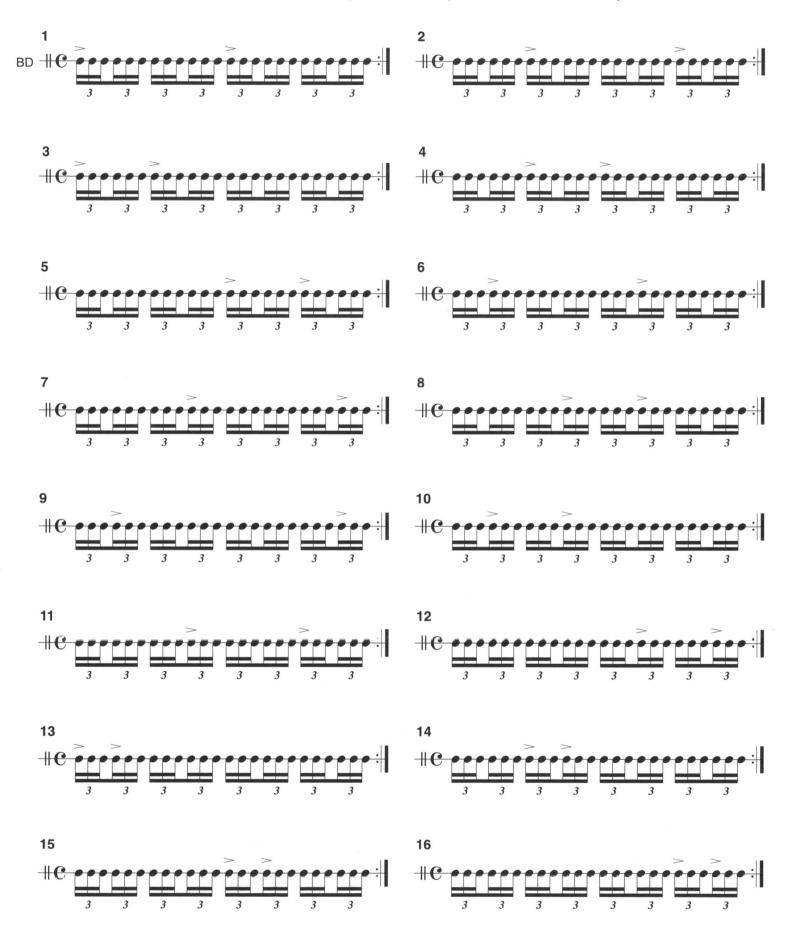

17
BD
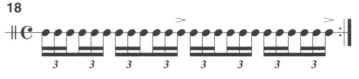

18
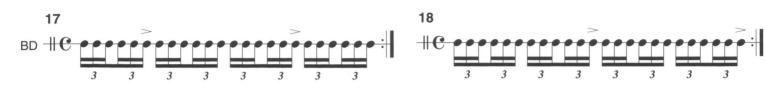

19
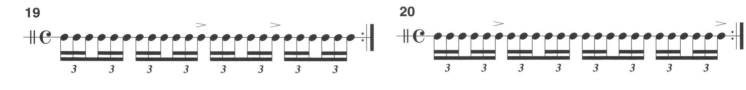

20
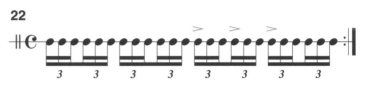

21
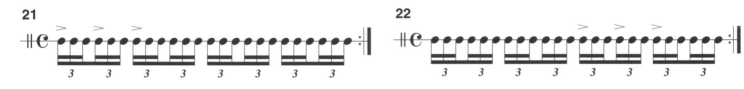

22
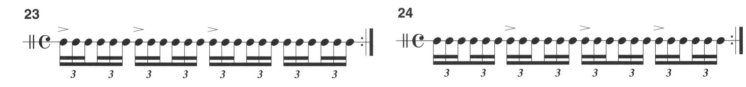

23

24
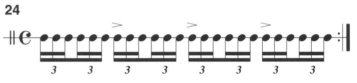

25
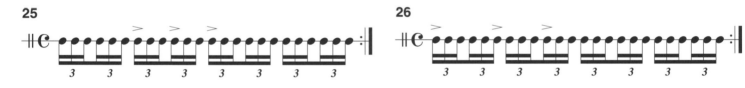

26
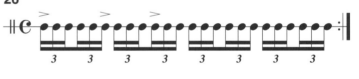

27
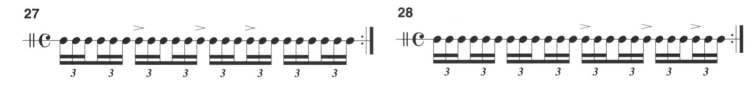

28

29
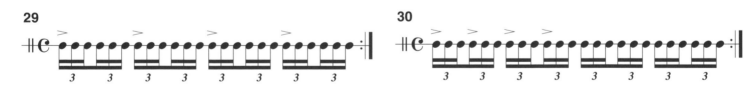

30

31
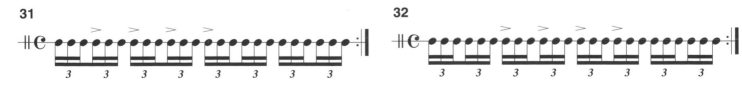

32
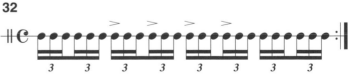

33

BD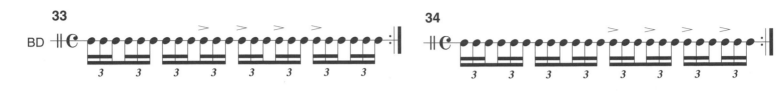

34

35

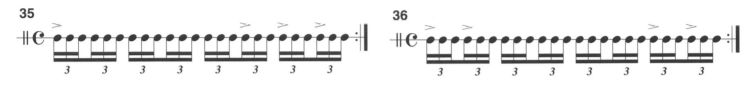

36

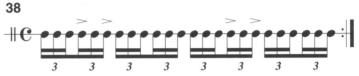

37

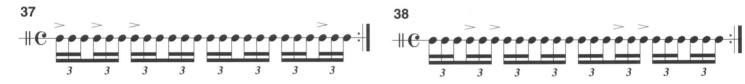

38

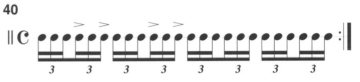

39

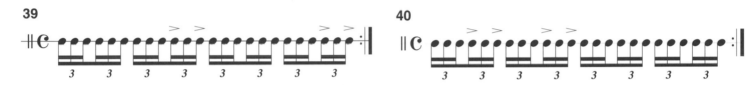

40

41

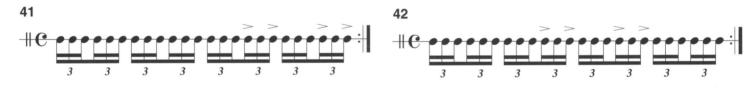

42

43

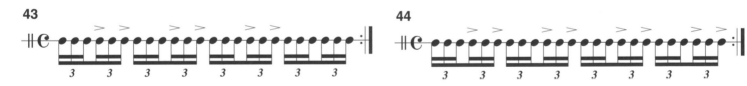

44

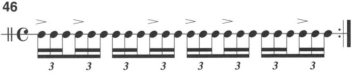

45

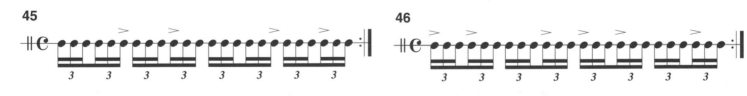

46

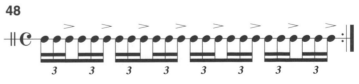

47

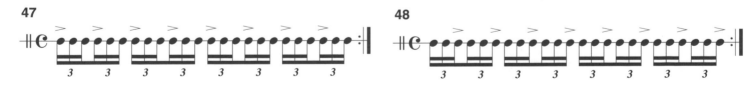

48

Part 3: 16th-Note-Triplet Bass Drum Solo

Part 3 is a bass drum solo that utilizes 16th-note triplets, 8th notes, quarter notes, and accents. Start slowly, increase the tempo gradually, and use a metronome or drum machine to keep a record of your progress.

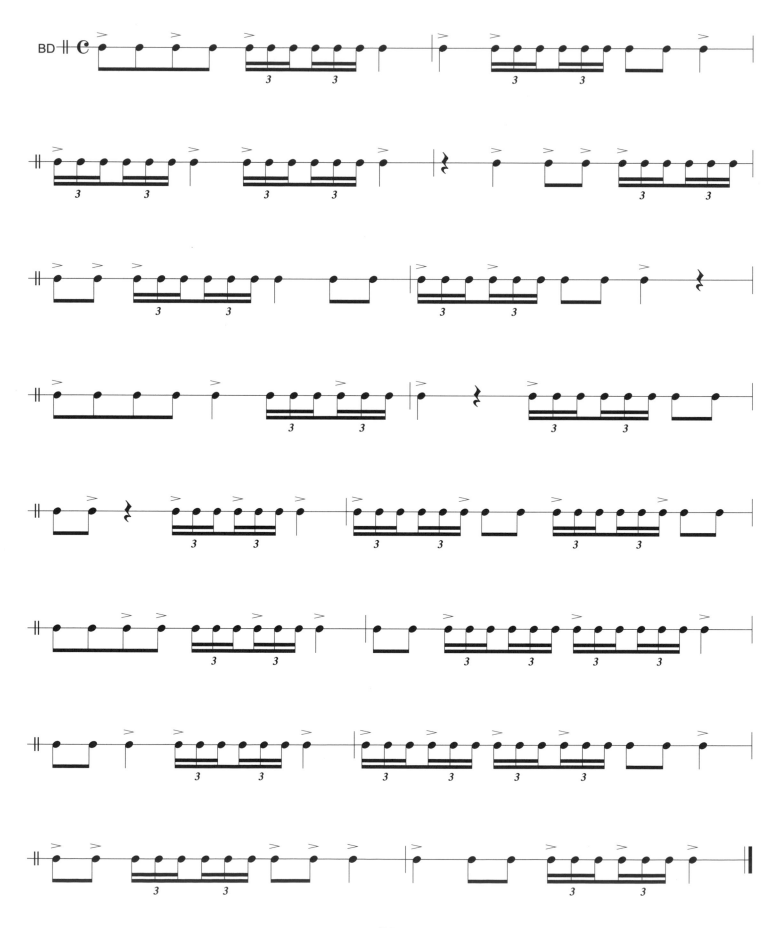

Part 4: 16th-Note-Triplet Hand And Foot Patterns

The patterns on the following four pages are built around hand and foot coordination with 16th-note triplets. The exercises become increasingly difficult as you work your way through. A slower tempo at the onset is recommended. Once again, the accents are optional.

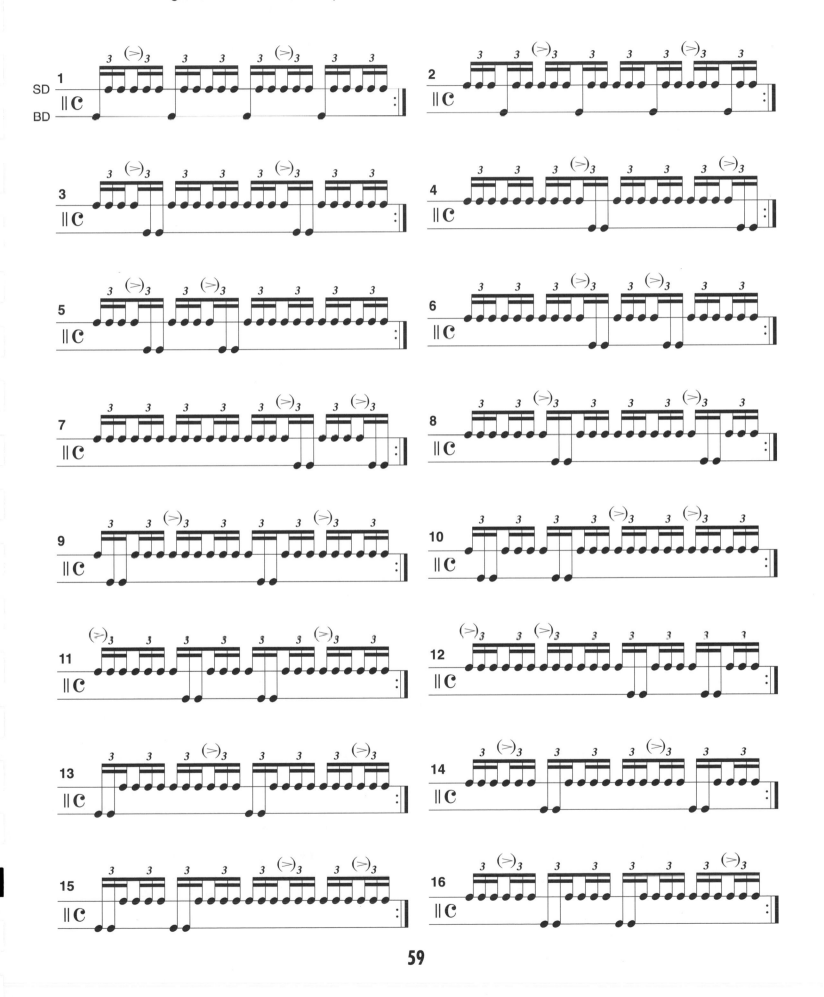

59

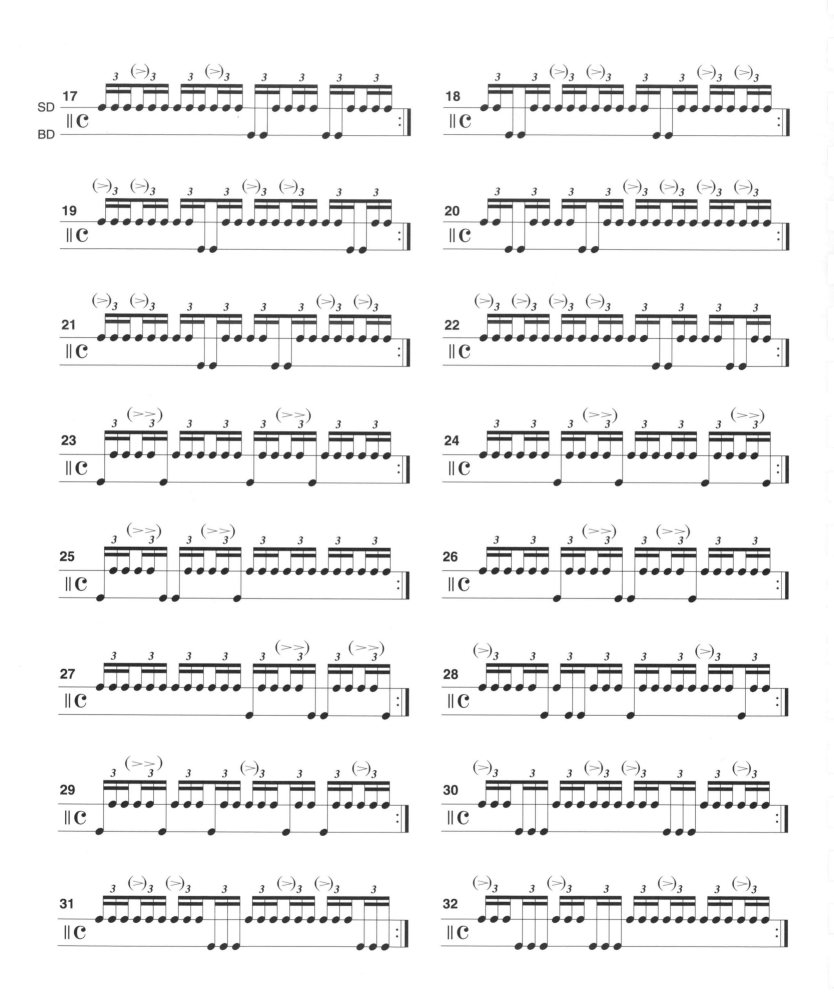

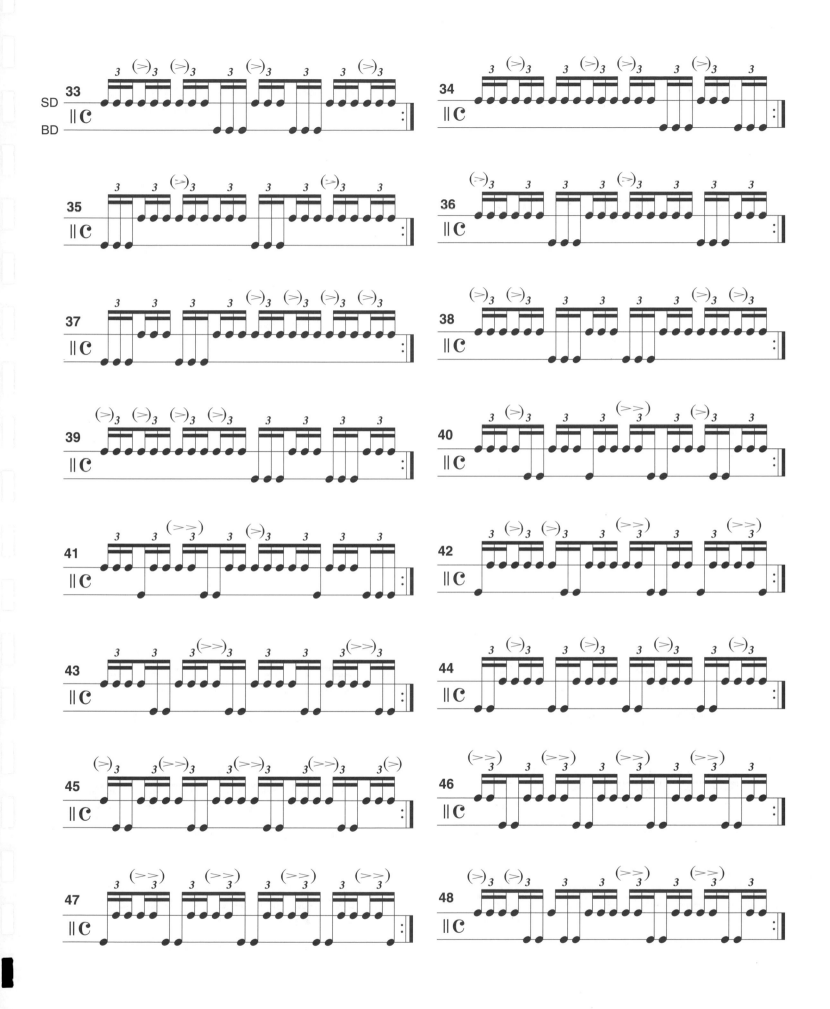

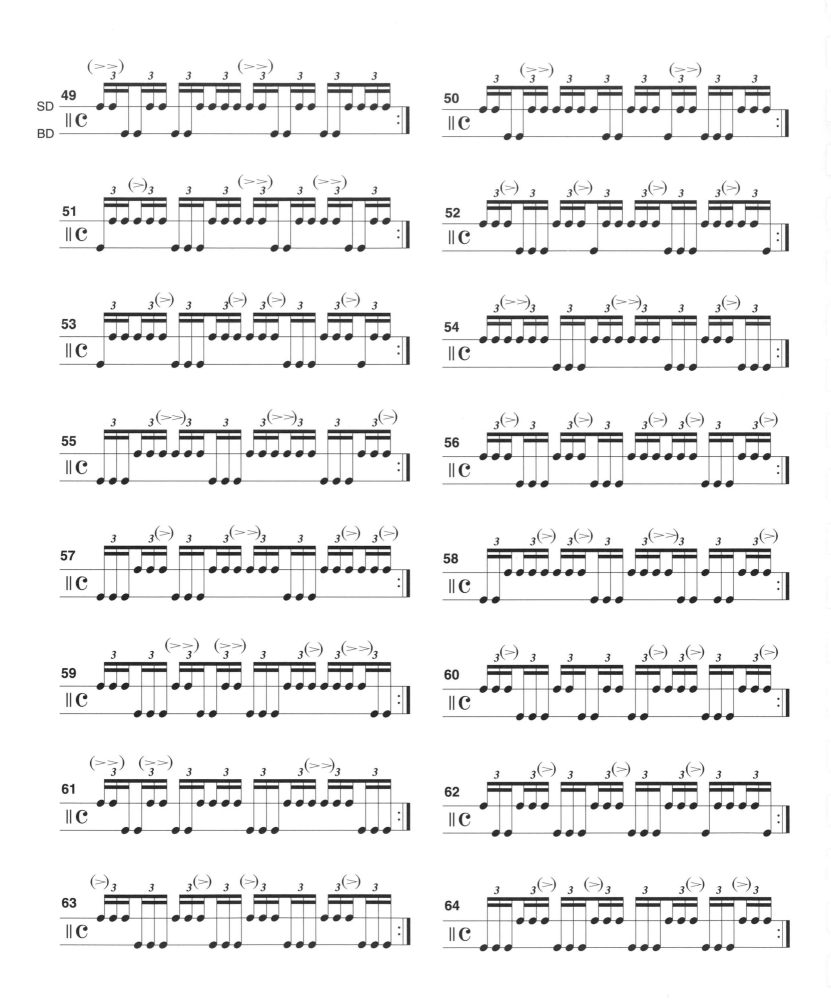

Part 5: 16th-Note-Triplet Hand And Foot Solo

Here's a sixteen-bar solo using most of the 16th-note-triplet hand and foot patterns studied on the previous four pages. Also note the wide use of accents throughout the solo. Practice slowly at first, and increase the speed once you become more familiar with the material. Do not consider this solo mastered until you can play it from beginning to end without a mistake.

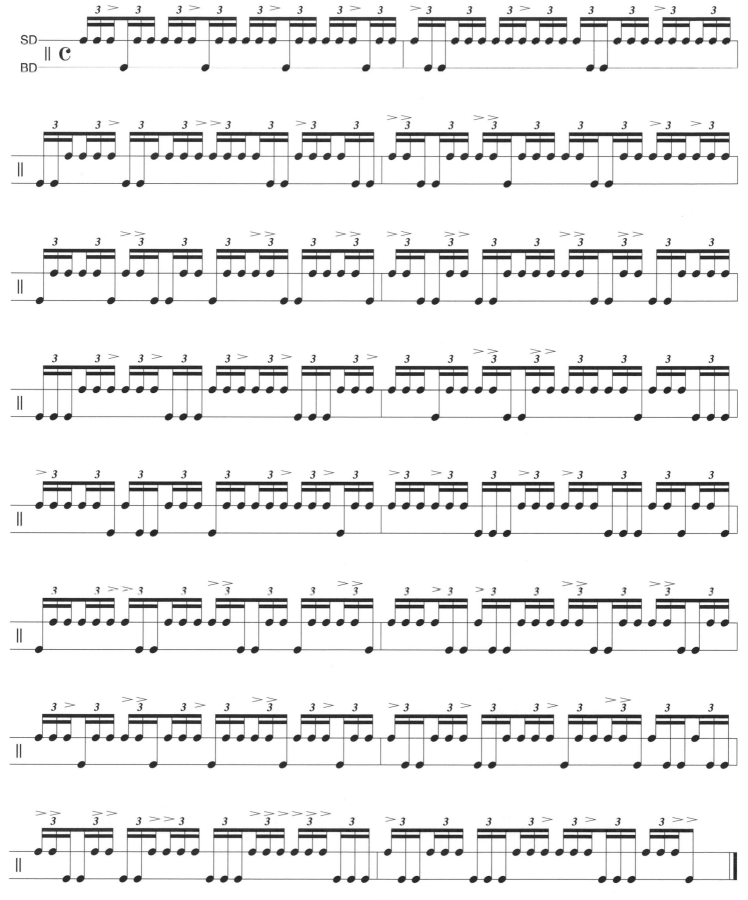

63

Section 7

Part 1: 32nd-Note Speed And Endurance Exercise

The purpose of Part 1 is to help you develop a greater degree of bass drum speed and endurance. Using 32nd notes, and starting at a comfortable tempo, play as many measures of 32nd notes as you can. Do not push to the point of cramping or burning. Stop when you can no longer control a full measure of 32nd notes.

On the Endurance Progress Chart below, you can keep a record of your progress on a daily or weekly basis in the Date column.

Start at a comfortable tempo and write that tempo down under the M.M. (metronome marking) column.

As you play each measure of 32nd notes, count out the total number of measures you are able to play without stopping, and mark it down in the Measures column.

The idea is to gradually increase both the speed (M.M.) and the number of measures you can play at that speed with each practice session. At the onset, *do not* attempt to play at a tempo faster than you're capable of playing. *Do not* attempt to play more measures than you can comfortably play. Foot speed, endurance, and control come with relaxed muscle action and gradual, consistent practice.

ENDURANCE PROGRESS CHART

Date	M.M.	# Of Measures

Part 2: 32nd Notes With Accents

This final section uses 32nd notes with accents interspersed. Playing accents among 32nd notes places the greatest demand on foot speed, endurance, and control. Repeat each exercise five to ten times, and be sure to rest between each one. Increased strength and endurance comes with relaxed muscle action and consistent practice.

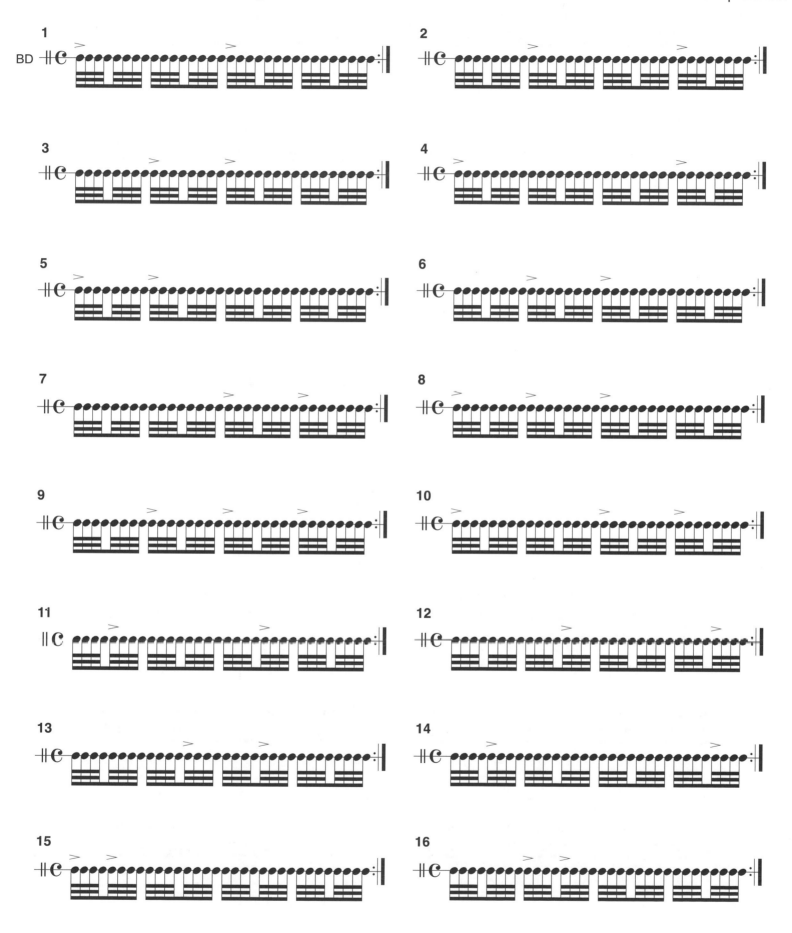

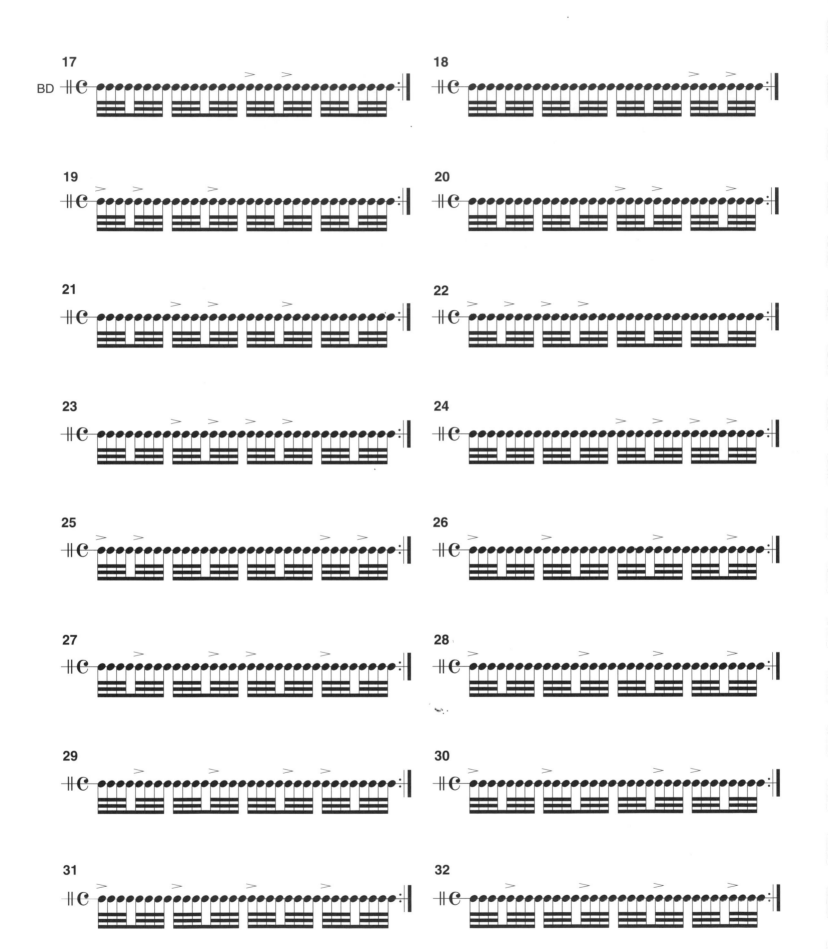

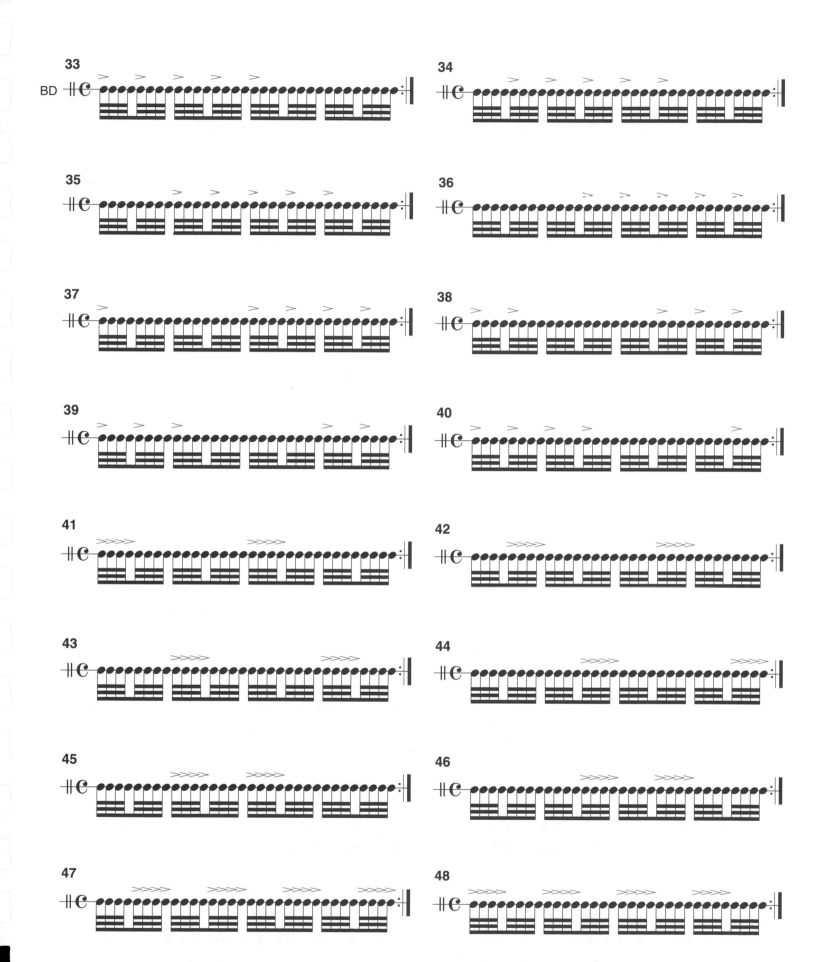

Part 3: 32nd-Note Bass Drum Solo

The solo here uses 32nd notes, 8ths, quarter notes, and accents interspersed. Be sure the accents stand out more strongly than the non-accented notes. Once again, take your time, and strive for accuracy and precise execution.

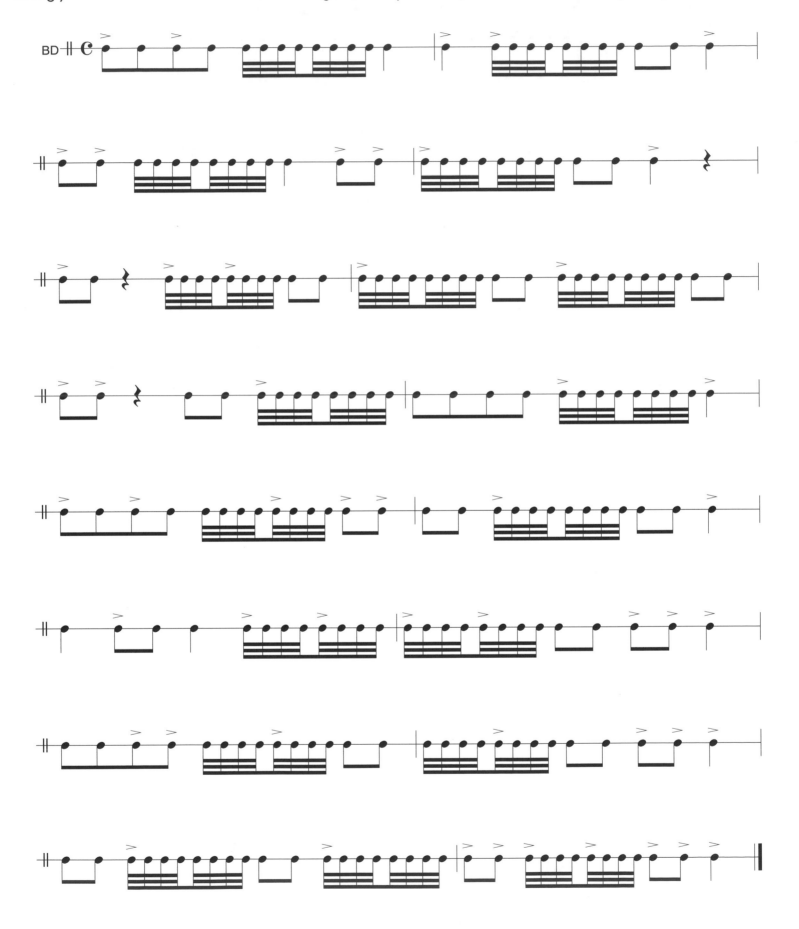

Part 4: 32nd-Note Hand And Foot Patterns

Playing hand and foot patterns with 32nd notes also places considerable demands on the foot. Try to play each pattern five to ten times without stopping. Start at a tempo where each exercise can be played smoothly and accurately, and increase the speed gradually with each practice session. Use a metronome to gauge your progress. After you've mastered each exercise, try moving the hand part around the various drums and cymbals on your kit.

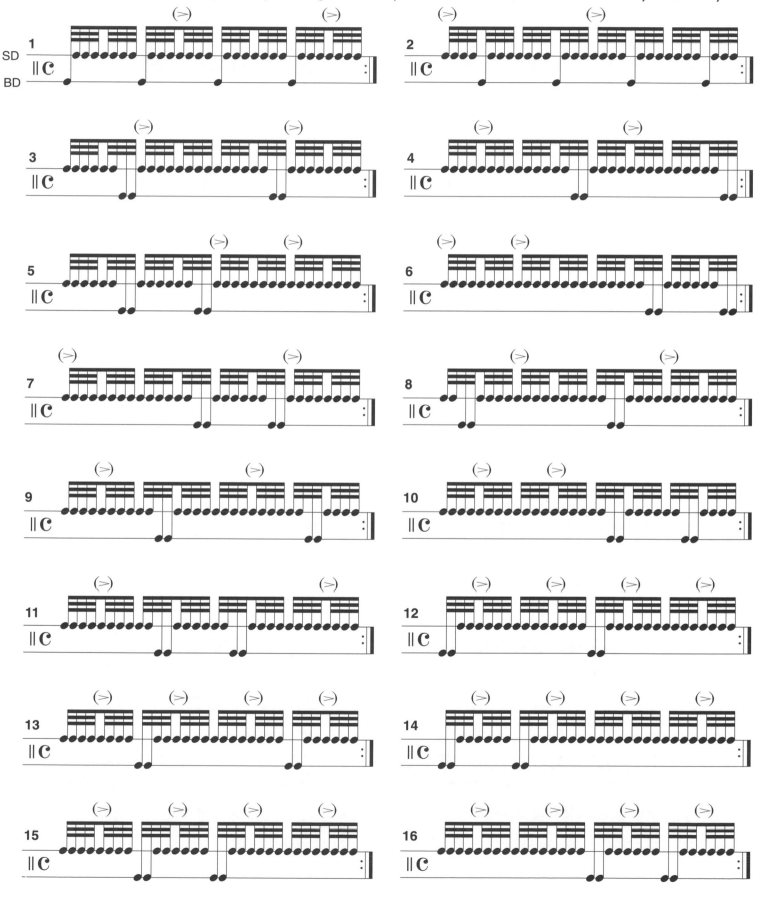

69

SD

BD

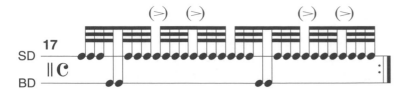
17

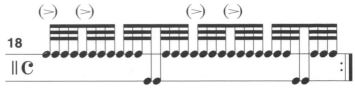
18

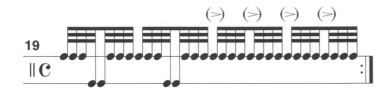
19

20

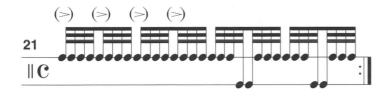
21

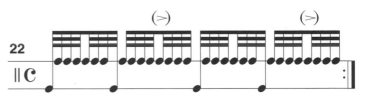
22

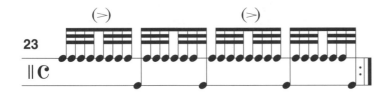
23

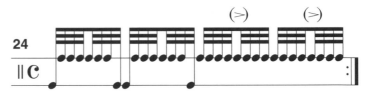
24

25

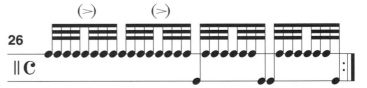
26

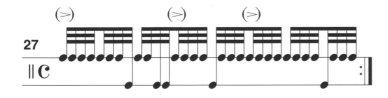
27

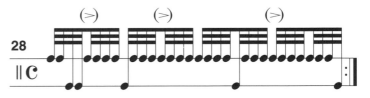
28

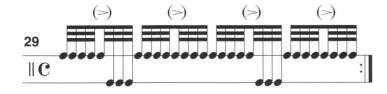
29

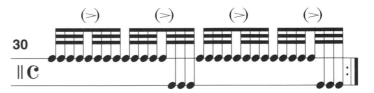
30

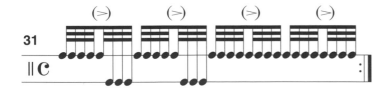
31

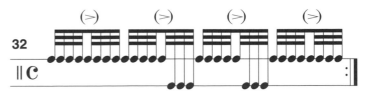
32

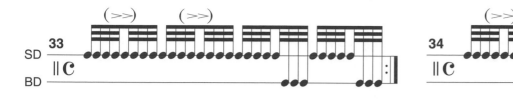
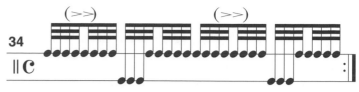
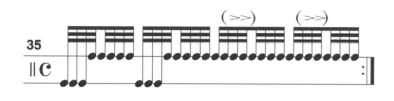
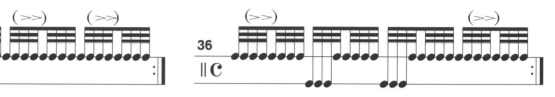
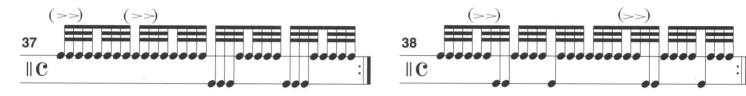
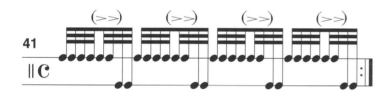
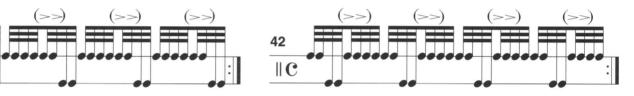
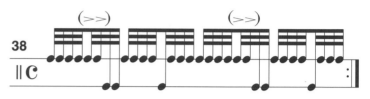
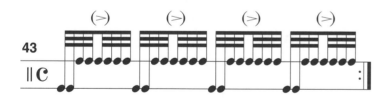
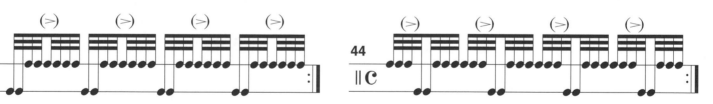
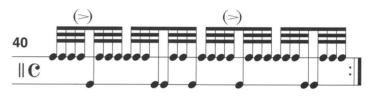
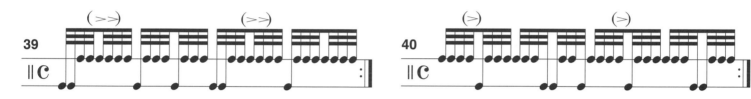
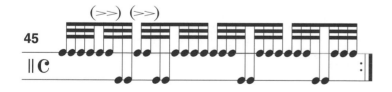
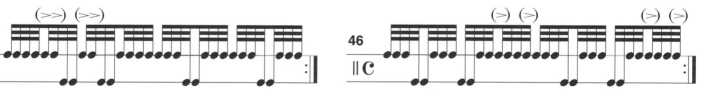
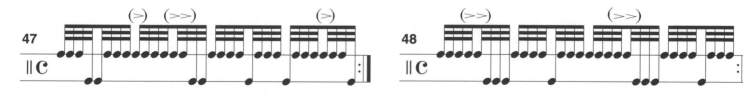
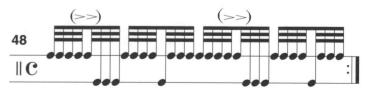

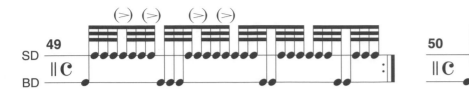

SD

BD

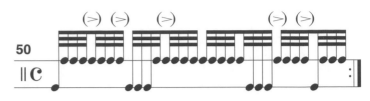

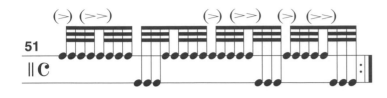

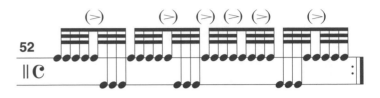

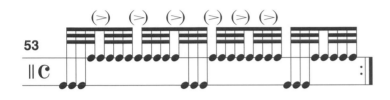

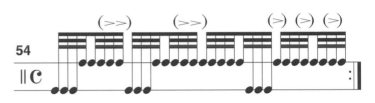

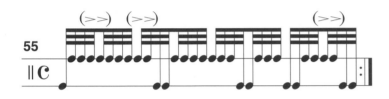

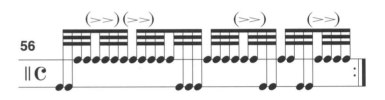

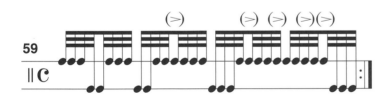

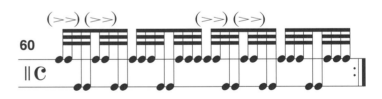

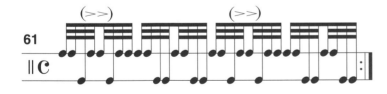

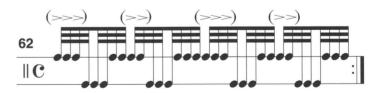

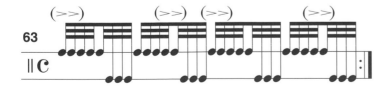

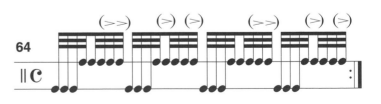

72

Part 5: 32nd-Note Hand And Foot Solo

Here's a sixteen-bar solo using most of the 32nd-note hand and foot patterns studied on the previous pages. The accents present an additional challenge. Increase the tempo only after you've become more familiar with the solo.

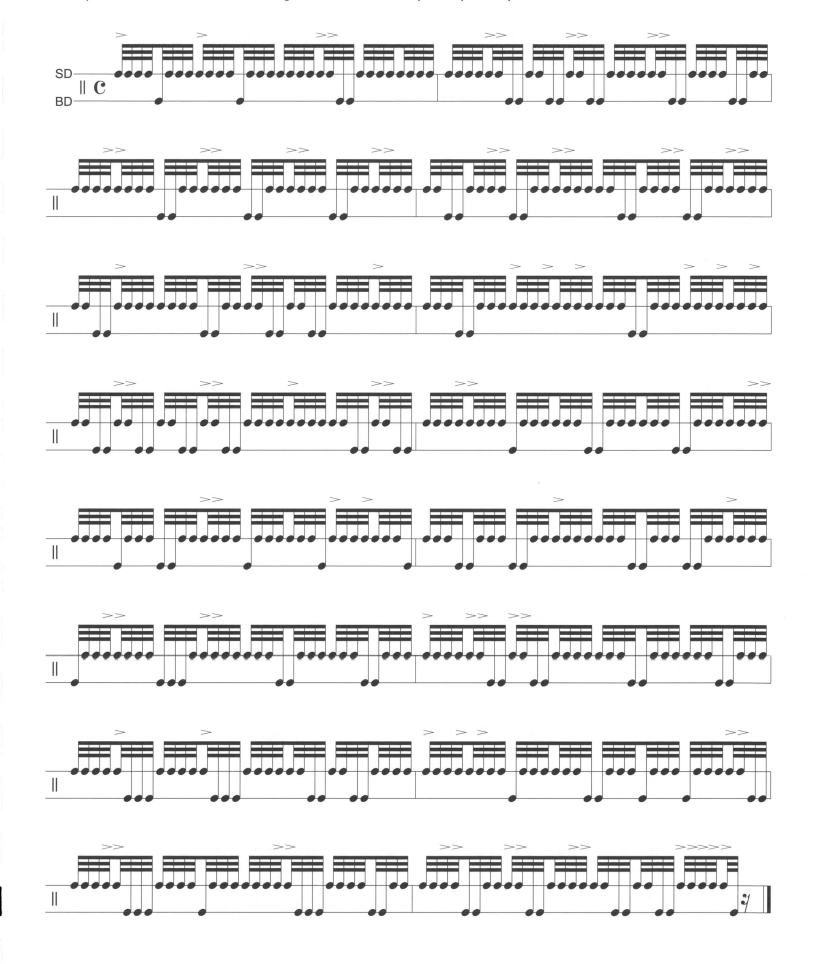

Section 8

Combination Solo Using 8th Notes And Triplets

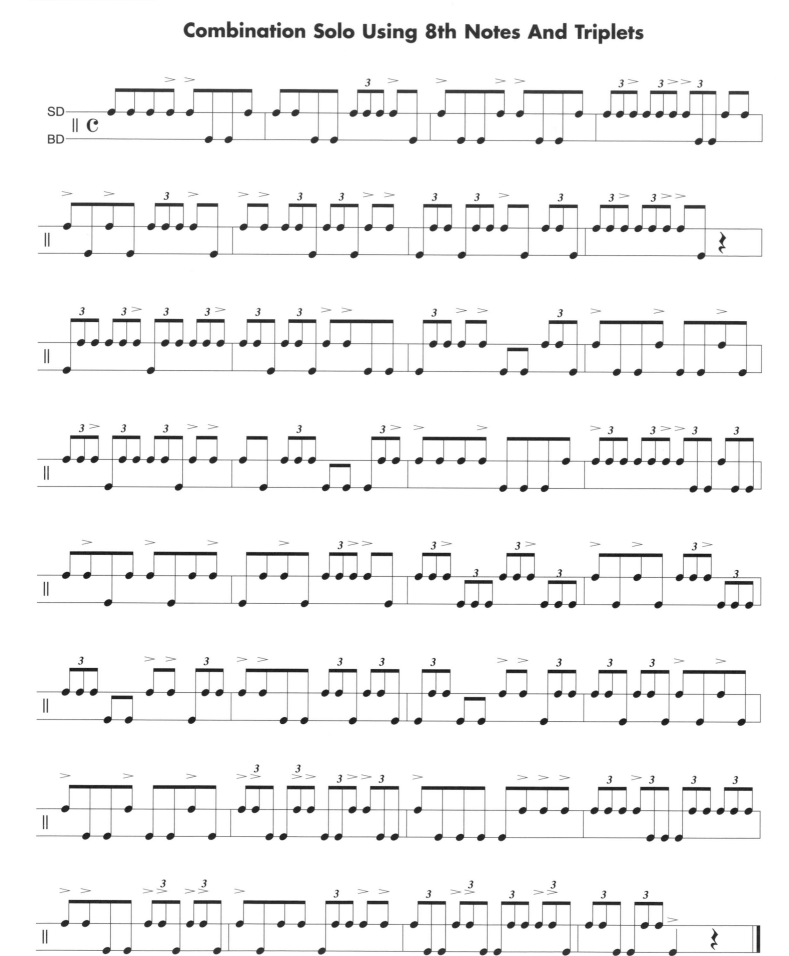

Combination Solo Using Triplets And 16th Notes

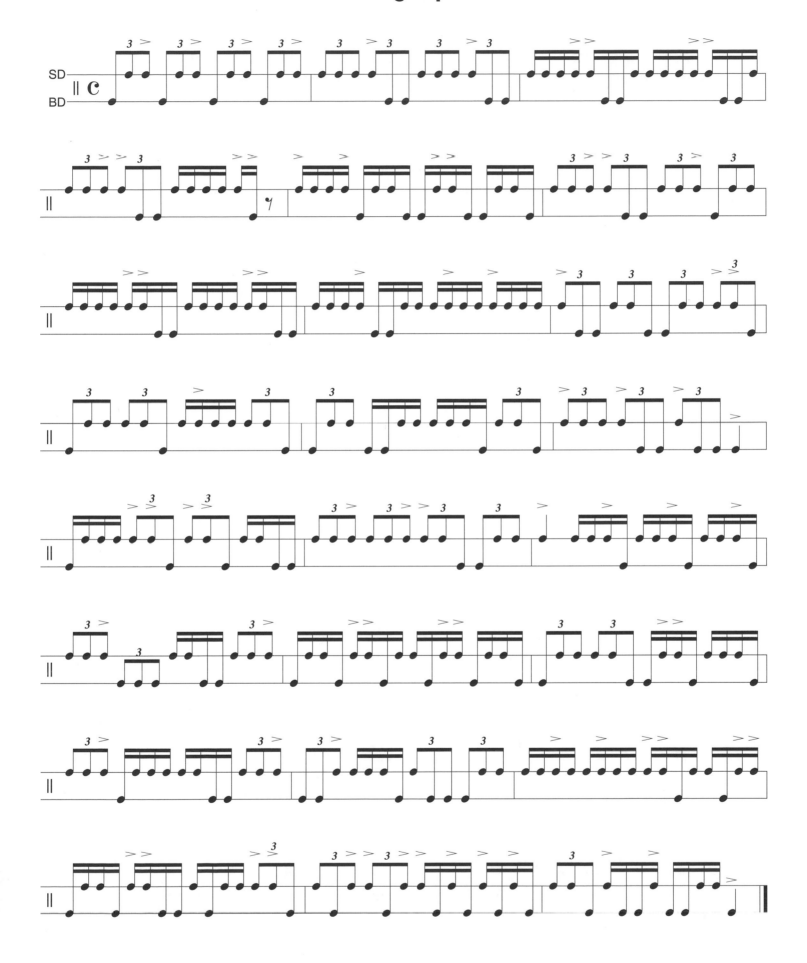

75

Combination Solo Using 16th-Note Figures 1 And 2

Combination Solo Using 16th Notes and 16th-Note Triplets

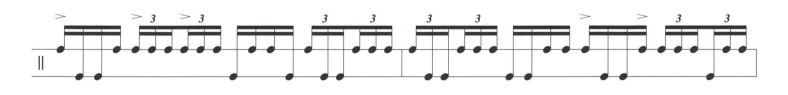

Combination Solo Using 16th-Note Triplets And 32nd Notes

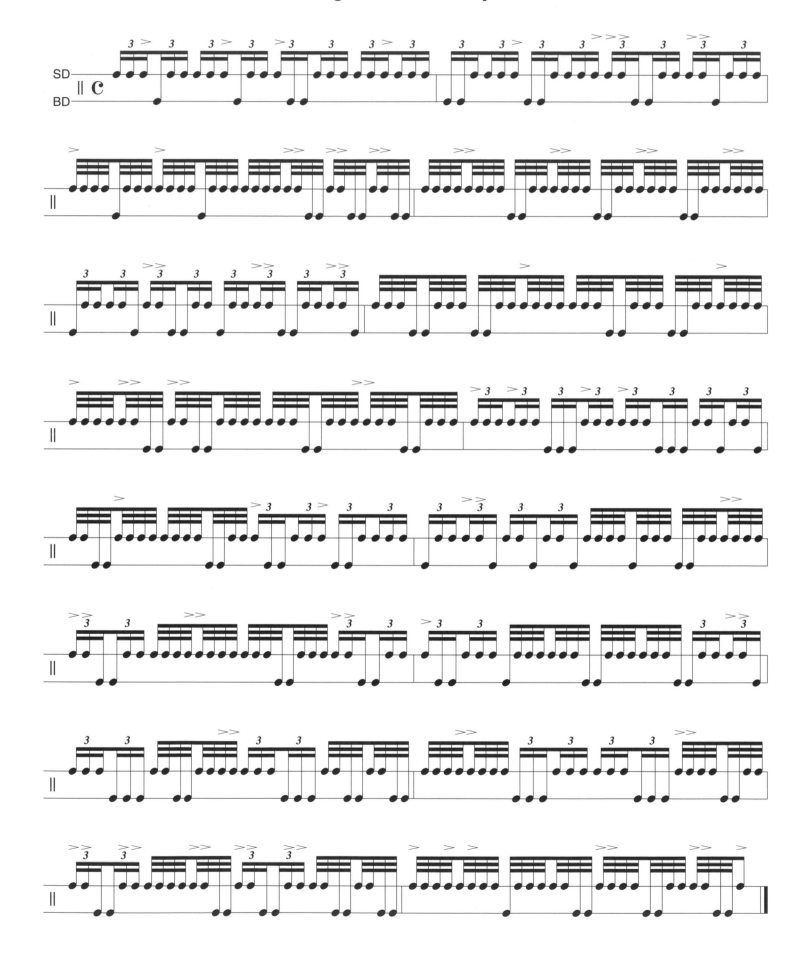

From Today's **Hot Young Players...**

...**Danny Carey** (Tool), **Taylor Hawkins** (Foo Fighters), **Ginger Fish** (Marilyn Manson), **Kevin Miller** (Fuel), **Tyler Stewart** (Barenaked Ladies), **Tré Cool** (Green Day), **Stefanie Eulinburg** (Kid Rock), **Tommy Stewart** (Godsmack), **Al 3** (Powerman 5000), **Dave Buckner** (Papa Roach), **Tony Fagenson** (Eve 6), **Paul Doucette** (Matchbox 20), **Samantha Maloney** (Hole/Mötley Crüe), **Jon Fishman** (Phish), **Abe Cunningham** (Deftones), **Greg Eklund** (Everclear), **sPaG** (Mudvayne)...

...To The **Legends Of Drumming...**

...Charlie Watts, Jim Keltner, Tito Puente, Steve Smith, Hal Blaine, Manu Katche, Glen Velez, Terry Bozzio, Peter Erskine, Will Kennedy, Jeff Hamilton, Simon Phillips, Richie Hayward, Roy Haynes, Zakir Hussain, Omar Hakim, Airto, Rod Morgenstein, Mel Lewis, Ricky Lawson, Billy Cobham, and more.

Young Drummers And Old. Hot New Players To Seasoned Veterans.

MODERN DRUMMER COVERS IT ALL!

Subcribe today! Mail the coupon below, or
subcribe online at www.moderndrummer.com

KEY CODE B-25

❑ **1 Year: $34.97** (SAVE 41% off the newsstand price)

❑ **2 Years: $56.97** (SAVE OVER 50% off the newsstand price)

❑ **Payment Enclosed**   ❑ **Bill Me**

❑ **MasterCard**   ❑ **Visa**

Card Number

Exp. Date

Signature

Name

Address

City

State   Zip

Phone (optional)

Mail to: Modern Drummer Publications
PO Box 480
Mt. Morris, IL 61054

Rates good in US, Canada, and Mexico. For foreign delivery send $41.97 for one year, $79.97 for two years (US currency only). Add an additional $75 per year for air-mail. Please allow 6–8 weeks for delivery.

THE MODERN DRUMMER LIBRARY

Master Studies
by Joe Morello

The book on hand development and drumstick control. *Master Studies* focuses on important aspects of drumming technique.
06631474 • $12.95

The Great American Drums
by Harry Cangany

The history of American drum manufacturing. A valuable collector's reference source.
06620010 • $19.95

The Drummer's Studio Survival Guide
by Mark Parsons

The definitive book on recording drums, for the novice to professional drummer.
00330257 • $12.95

The Drummer's Time
by Rick Mattingly

A compilation of enlightening conversations with the great drummers of jazz, from Louie Bellson to Tony Williams.
00330454 • $12.95

The Modern Snare Drummer
by Ron Spagnardi

38 exciting solos for the intermediate to advanced snare drummer that challenge both reading and technical skills. Perfect for percussion majors and as audition and contest pieces.
00330458 • $12.95

The Encyclopedia of Double Bass Drumming
by Bobby Rondinelli & Michael Lauren

Designed to improve your double bass playing ability, this progressive book focuses on developing a comprehensive double bass drum or double pedal drumming style. Incorporates a variety of styles including rock, funk, and blues.
06620037 • $12.95

Applied Rhythms 06630365 • $8.95	**Great Jazz Drummers** 06621755 • $19.95	**The New Breed** 06631619 • $12.95
Best of Concepts 06621766 • $9.95	**Electronic Drummer** 06631500 • $9.95	**The Working Drummer** 00330264 • $14.95
Best of Modern Drummer: Rock 06621759 • $9.95	**Progressive Independence** 00330290 • $12.95	**Cross-Sticking Studies** 00330377 • $12.95
When in Doubt, Roll 06630298 • $13.95	**Drum Wisdom** 06630510 • $7.95	

* Prices, contents and availability are subject to change without notice.

FOR MORE INFORMATION, SEE YOUR LOCAL MUSIC DEALER,
OR WRITE TO:

HAL•LEONARD® CORPORATION

7777 W. BLUEMOUND RD. P.O. BOX 13819 MILWAUKEE, WI 53213
WWW.HALLEONARD.COM

0401